Ida M. Holson

Jan. 1932.

PSYCHOLOGY AT WORK

PSYCHOLOGY

at

WORK

by

LOIS HAYDEN MEEK
FLOYD H. ALLPORT
MORRIS S. VITELES
WALTER R. MILES
ARTHUR I. GATES
ARNOLD GESELL
MARK A. MAY

Edited by

PAUL S. ACHILLES

WHITTLESEY HOUSE
McGRAW-HILL BOOK COMPANY, INC.
NEW YORK AND LONDON
1932

Published by

WHITTLESEY HOUSE
A Division of the
McGraw-Hill Book Company, Inc.

Printed in the United States of America by
The Maple Press Company, York, Pa.

LIST OF CONTRIBUTORS

FLOYD H. ALLPORT, Professor of Social and Political Psychology, School of Citizenship and Public Affairs, Syracuse University.

ARTHUR I. GATES, Professor of Educational Psychology, Teachers College, Columbia University.

ARNOLD GESELL, Director, Clinic of Child Development, Yale University.

MARK A. MAY, Professor of Educational Psychology and Executive Secretary, Institute of Human Relations, Yale University.

LOIS HAYDEN MEEK, Director, Child Development Institute Teachers College, Columbia University.

WALTER R. MILES, Professor of Experimental Psychology, Stanford University, Visiting Professor of Psychiatry and Psychology, School of Medicine, Yale University.

MORRIS S. VITELES, Assistant Professor of Psychology, University of Pennsylvania.

The material for this volume was derived from a series of lectures on Psychology and Its Useful Applications arranged by the Psychological Corporation and delivered under its auspices in New York City during the winter of 1931.

FOREWORD

In primitive times, before scientific study of natural processes had progressed far enough to be of much service in manufacturing and engineering, the practical man had to depend on rule of thumb, which was based on experience to a certain extent and which worked fairly well in carrying on the old, familiar processes. But things often went wrong, and the primitive tribe was much inclined to lend its ear to the man of magic, who asserted his ability to get results by the aid of his magic wand or incantations. The magician could not explain *how* the results issued from his procedures, but appealed to the love of mystery which still seems to be strong in many of us.

Later emerged the man of science, who saw no virtue whatever in mystery. He wished to dispel mystery as fast as he could. He wished to trace out the processes of cause and effect. When he had traced out a natural process, he was in a position to secure effects by providing the appropriate causes. In engineering and more recently in medicine, science has carried the day against rule of thumb and magic.

In human behavior there is much that is still obscure; the processes are not yet traced out as completely as in physics and chemistry—and even in those older sciences a vast deal remains for further investigation. We have to be patient with science, just because her job is so vast and so difficult. But, as the practical man has to carry on in some way, he seizes on the most promising guidance available. Along comes the man of magic, even as in the old days, claiming great efficacy for certain mysterious procedures of his own. He says he can read character from

[vii]

the curves of the face or from the lines of the hand or even from the star under which a person was born. If we ask him to explain the connection between the stars and human doings, he says it is all a mystery. The chances are that such mysteries contain nothing at all that is genuine.

Nowhere is patience more necessary than with the science of psychology. Its job is bound to be long and difficult. Accordingly you will find the claims of scientific psychologists at the present time to be decidedly moderate. They are not "claiming the earth" by any manner of means. Yet it is remarkable how useful some of their discoveries are in practical life. Scientific investigation of human behavior and development has already produced usable results, and is adding more every year.

ROBERT S. WOODWORTH,
Professor of Psychology, Columbia University;
Past President, The Psychological Corporation.

NEW YORK,
December, 1931.

PREFACE

This book differs in character from the usual presentations of psychology. With no pretense of completeness as a treatise it portrays in a series of brief sketches some of the interesting and significant things that psychologists have done and are doing. The result is a realistic picture of the science at work, affording the reader quick acquaintance with its aims and uses, its problems and methods, and above all, its exacting requirements as a science.

Changes wrought in our daily affairs by discoveries and technological advances in other sciences are generally more apparent and acceptable than those arising from psychology. Compare, for example, our reactions to radios and to intelligence tests. These two products of science have come upon us almost contemporaneously and now play important parts in the modern scene. But while radios bring us news of the world and its wares, tests only tell us about ourselves. It is true that the capacities which such tests measure cannot always be definitely defined, but the significance of what they measure cannot be denied. Nor can the fact that we need to have and to face more scientific knowledge about ourselves if we are to adapt ourselves successfully to the products of a scientific era.

With our material progress our troubles and social maladjustments seem to multiply instead of diminish. The physicists, the chemists, and the engineers set a fast pace for our slow-changing habits. Like Pandora they have opened the box, and now books such as "Business Adrift," "Whither Mankind," "Toward Civilization," and "The Way to Recovery" typify our plight and plead for planning and leadership to save us. It is not likely that we shall be so lacking in courage and adaptability as to forego the scientific method and close the lid, but rather that the fairy of Hope may eventually emerge through applying the scientific method to the study of man. At least it is not presumptuous to say that psychology hopes to contribute helpfully in the synthesis of sciences and the social planning now indicated as essential to our welfare. Evidence of such contributions is found in this book. Let me illustrate with a single instance.

On the way to the publishers with the first draft of the manuscript for the volume, I passed a parade of garment workers on strike in the mid-town district of New York. The slogan on one of their placards epitomized our social maladjustments. It read, "Down with the inhuman speed-up system." A deeper challenge to psychologists than to employers, yet placement of the blame on any shoulders would be impossible. What heartened me were the specific references to this very "system" in the manuscript beneath my arm, showing that psychologists were already at work on such problems with a spirit and with techniques of greater promise than strikes and slogans.

The Editor's small part in the compilation of this volume consisted chiefly in the arrangement of a series of lectures, under auspices of the Psychological Corporation, from which the book developed. In this he was encouraged by Dr. James McKeen Cattell, who, in 1921, founded the Psychological Corporation for the advancement of psychology and the promotion of its useful applications. To him and to the contributors all credit is due. Invaluable assistance at many points from initiation of the lectures to completion of the book was rendered by Dr. Elsie O. Bregman and Miss Wilhelmina Bennett. The Editor speaks for the contributors in gratefully acknowledging many permissions from authors and publishers both in this country and abroad for use of their materials and in extending full recognition and thanks to all whose work in psychology has made this book possible.

PAUL S. ACHILLES.

NEW YORK,
December, 1931.

CONTENTS

[xiii]

PSYCHOLOGY AT WORK

Chapter I

PSYCHOLOGY AND THE PRESCHOOL CHILD

by Lois Hayden Meek

Early Beginnings

FOR many years psychologists and educators have been studying children. One of the first scientific studies of children was made in 1781 by D. Tiedemann who made observations of his infant child. Little further progress was made however, until the latter part of the nineteenth century when W. Preyer in Germany and Millicent Shinn in the United States led a large group of enthusiastic men and women to study children by keeping diary records of their own babies. At about the same time, G. Stanley Hall introduced the questionnaire as a method of collecting information about children. Through these biographies and questionnaires a great deal of material was brought together which had some influence on education.

Three men during the present century have greatly influenced the studying of children. Alfred Binet in France developed a test to measure mental status or ability and thereby gave to psychologists a tool for study which has greatly increased our understanding of children. Edward L. Thorndike and John B. Watson, by the close of the second decade of the century had introduced us to the study of children through the experimental method. With this background of biography, questionnaire, mental testing, and experimental procedure, the psychological study of children during the past decade has made great strides.

[3]

Influence of Related Movements

The present movement toward the psychological study of preschool children has been influenced by psychology and also by three parallel movements: child health, mental hygiene, and education. The child-health movement during the last twenty-five years has shown very clearly not only that the preschool years are important developmentally, but also that the influence of parents and home upon a child's physical development is significant. Infant mortality statistics show that in 1928, sixty-nine of every thousand infants born alive died during the first year; and that 15.7 per cent of all deaths occur below five years of age. Studies of the physical defects in preschool children have shown that there is less than a 50 per cent chance that a child will complete the preschool years sound in body. Defects in teeth, tonsils, nasal breathing, and nutrition are the most prevalent defects which are preventable and which may have far-reaching effects on later growth and development.[1]

The mental hygiene movement since its beginnings early in the twentieth century has continually shown the need for studies of normal emotional growth. Beginning as a movement for the prevention of adult psychopathology, interest and attention in the field has gradually pushed to lower and lower levels: to juvenile delinquency, to behavior problems of school children, to preschool problems.

[1] The following references report surveys which have been made of the physical status of children:

BAKER, S. JOSEPHINE, "Child Hygiene," pp. xii, 534 (pp. 225, 255–257), New York, Harper & Brothers, 1925.

ROBERTS, LYDIA J., "Children of Preschool Age in Gary, Indiana," (Part II Diet of Children), pp. 53–170, Washington, D. C., Children's Bureau, U. S. Department of Labor, 1925.

ROBERTS, LYDIA J., "Nutrition Work with Children," pp. xiv, 394, Chicago, University of Chicago Press, 1927.

RUDE, A. D., "Physical Status of Preschool Children, Gary, Indiana," pp. 84, Washington, D. C., Children's Bureau, U. S. Department of Labor, 1924.

Records from juvenile court studies as well as from behavior clinics have emphasized the importance of early behavior manifestations and the influence of home and parents.

Developments in education during this quarter century have also had a decided influence on the trends in child study today. Among these developments are the modern kindergarten with its emphasis on child activity, creative materials, motor development, freedom of movement; the modern progressive school with its program for guidance of children in learning and living in all life's activities; the movement for education of preschool children and the consequent growth of nursery schools; home economics with its concern for the home as the center of child life and for parent-child relationships; parent education with its demand for facts and information usable and helpful to parents. Certainly these trends in education have created a need and a demand for scientific information which may be used as a basis for the guidance of children.

Present Research Activities

The present movement, therefore, in the study of children might logically be called a movement for the study of the development and guidance of children. There are four outstanding characteristics of present research:

1. It is a study of normal children.

2. It is genetic in its approach.

3. It attempts to integrate the contributions of such related fields as: nutrition, medicine, anthropometry, education, mental hygiene, and psychology.

4. It attempts to build up facts that are usable by parents and others engaged in the guidance of children.

Some of the most outstanding work in the study of preschool development is being conducted in institutes connected with universities. Such institutes are located at the University of Minnesota; the University of Iowa; Teachers College, Columbia University; the University of California; Yale University; Johns Hopkins University; University of Toronto and McGill University in Canada. The Merrill-Palmer School in Detroit and the Washington Child Research Center in Washington, D. C., are independent units established for similar purposes. In addition there are many other places in the United States at which studies of children are being made. A recent survey shows a total of 641 investigators in the field of child development of whom 238 are psychologists.[2]

One of the interesting trends of the modern movement in child study has been the use of the nursery school as a laboratory for research. In fact, the nursery school has developed parallel with the movement for the study of preschool children. All of the research centers mentioned above conduct nursery schools. Nursery schools enroll children from about eighteen months to about four years of age. Usually, though not always, the age range in any one group is from one to two years. In the nursery schools at the Child Development Institute of Teachers College, Columbia University, there are two groups of children, the younger having an age range from about eighteen months to two and one-half years, the older from two and one-half years to three and one-half years. The number of children in nursery school groups varies from about fifteen to twenty-four. The groups at the Institute have respectively eighteen and twenty children in each. For these groups there are one head teacher and two assistant teachers.

The program of the nursery school makes possible a broad contact with children and gives an opportunity to study them from many different aspects of development. The daily program consists of morning inspection by the

[2] These figures were secured from Dr. Allen Hicks, National Research Council, Washington, D. C.

nurse, outdoor play, mid-morning lunch, toileting, main midday meal, nap, and afternoon lunch. This gives an opportunity for the study of children during the important activities of their lives: playing, sleeping, eating, dressing, and eliminating. We see them when they separate from their parents, when they play in groups with other children their own age, and we see them in their relations with the several adults in the nursery school. Children in the nursery schools of the Institute are given routine medical and psychological examinations. Records are made of anthropometric measurements, dietary intake, sickness, sleep, elimination, behavior habits, emotional adjustments, etc.

The purposes of the nursery school are to furnish an environment conducive to the best development of children; to offer an opportunity for parent education and guidance; and to provide facilities for research in child development and guidance.

The studies which have come from these nursery school laboratories during the past ten years are many and varied, including such topics as physical growth, nutrition, mental growth, habit formation, behavior problems, social development, language and play activities.

Behavior of Preschool Children

In general, the behavior during the first six years of life is characterized by rapid change, great activity, great learning. A comparison of a newborn babe with a six-year-old child tells the tale of rapid change in behavior, a change greater than in any subsequent six years of life. Gesell[3] describes the behavior of a newborn babe a few hours after birth.

While he lies in his crib before he is lifted out for his first bath he is busily engaged in making mouthing movements. He turns

[3] GESELL, ARNOLD, "The Mental Growth of the Pre-School Child," pp. x, 447 (pp. 199–201), New York, The Macmillan Company, 1925.

[7]

his head with almost rhythmic regularity at about forty-five degrees. He yawns from time to time with amazing expertness and apparently with all the skill of an adult. His eyes continually move back and forth with a slow semi-rhythmic regularity. He cries momentarily, apparently not from any distress, about six times within a period of five minutes. His fingers are active and move independently, assuming many positions. At one time his thumb is curled inward; his index finger is sharply flexed, his little finger is sharply extended; and the ring and middle fingers in intermediate positions. The examiner tries to duplicate this postural arrangement of the fingers in his own hand and is unable to do so. The baby is mildly startled if his mattress is suddenly pushed against his back, but he is not startled by a loud sound.

Mild vocalization is sharply increased when he is lifted onto the table for the ministrations of the nurse. The vocalization is as sharply concluded as soon as he is allowed to rest free on the table surface. It is renewed as soon as the nurse begins to wash and wipe the eyes. There are definite head aversion movements and an increase of leg movements. There is a quieting down while the neck and body are cleaned. There is facial and bodily squirming when the baby is lifted from the table into the weighing pan, but random movements resume as soon as he is laid down. The great toe displays a surprising mobility and remains separated for a few moments by as much as one centimeter and one-half from the adjacent toe. When the baby is placed on the table he tolerates the prone position; he flexes his legs in a manner which simulates mild crawling movements. His right cheek, however, rests with a hapless heaviness upon the table top. He closes his right eye protectively while in this position, but his left eye is wide open. He cannot erect his head to relieve any discomfort from his head posture, if indeed he feels discomfort at all. He cries again lustily for a brief moment when the nurse begins to shampoo him, but he does not cry during the process of shampooing. Indeed it appears that he cries at the moment when there is a marked transition from one condition to another as though he were protesting against the transition rather than the result itself. He protests against the constraint that goes with

[8]

putting on the first garment but relaxes wih evident motor expansiveness when replaced snugly in his crib after this, his first bath and first dressing.

His facial expression takes on an aspect of increased alertness; there is a mild vocalization expressive of organic satisfaction. His lips resume their previous activity; his mouth closes and opens about a dozen times a minute; he sneezes, yawns, and falls to sleep.

If we compare these initial squirmings and unorganized movements of a newborn with the behavior of a six-year-old we find that the child has gradually learned to focus his eyes, to reach for an object, to grasp, to hold, to carry to his mouth, to shake, to pat, to throw, to pull, to build, to cut, to make, to sew, to hammer, to saw, to dig, to pour, to handle— in short to manipulate most of the things in his own enviroment to his own satisfaction. From a helpless infant who cannot hold up his head or turn his body, he has grown before school age in postural control to sit, to crawl, to stand erect, to walk, to run, to climb, to hop, skip and jump, to guide a kiddy-car, a tricycle, and mayhap to dance and swim. To his first reactions in tasting, feeling, hearing, and seeing he has added multitudes of experiences which have built for him a simple and usable understanding of most of the things in his environment. His birth cry and vocalizations will have developed into a vocabulary of some fifteen hundred to three thousand words.

These are only a few of the changes which take place so rapidly during the preschool years but they show the necessity for parents and others in charge of young children continually to adjust their standards for a child's behavior to his rapid development. Moreover, since this is the first period in a child's life it carries with it the weight of primacy. The behavior of children during this period will have important bearing on later behavior because it comes first and therefore all later experiences are based upon it.

[9]

This does not imply a fatalistic philosophy toward later development. It does not mean that what is learned during these years will necessarily always be the behavior of an individual. It does however, definitely lead to the conclusion that later learnings are based upon this early behavior and that the behavior will tend to persist throughout life unless other experiences occur to change it.

Scales of Mental Development.—One of the most important problems in the study of mental development is the measurement of intelligence. In order to know how intelligent any child is, it is necessary, of course, to know what other children of his age can do—to have an average or norm with which to compare him. If most five-year-old children can lace their shoes and your child cannot, then you can be pretty sure either that he is below the normal in this ability or that you have not given him adequate opportunity or proper guidance to learn to lace his shoes. If, however, we find that he not only is below his age group in lacing shoes but also in many other matters such as vocabulary, understanding of directions, memory, and drawing, we can be rather sure that he is low in mental development. It is important to know how a child stands in mental development in order that we may plan the best program for his education and guidance. It is also important that we be able to tell in advance what his future development will be— will he always be below average? To be able to prognosticate a child's development is most useful in cases of adoption as well as in educational guidance.

It is only within the last few years that we have had any tests which would help us to understand the mental development of infants. Studies tracing the monthly growth and development of infants have been made by several investigators, among whom are Arnold Gesell of Yale and Charlotte Buehler of Vienna. Buehler[4] has built a

[4] BUEHLER, CHARLOTTE, "The First Year of Life," pp. x, 281, New York, John Day Company, 1930.

[10]

scale of performances for children month by month for the first two years of life. The items in this scale were taken from actual observations of infants' behavior. Gesell[5] studied infants in his clinic by comparing the behavior of infants of various ages and has built a scale of development from one month to five years. The items of the scale are classified into motor development, language, adaptive behavior, and personal-social behavior. Many of the particular items are extended over several months and give an excellent basis for comparing different stages of development. For example, under motor development the items referring to control of head give us a picture of what to expect of normal babies at different ages:

One month—Lifts head from time to time when held to the shoulder; lifts head intermittently, though unsteadily, when in prone position; turns head laterally when in prone position.

Two months—Holds head erect for a short time when held to the shoulder; lifts head when suspended dorsally (the head being momentarily unsupported to test the compensatory postural adjustment).

Three months—Holds head erect and steady when held to shoulder.

Four months—Holds head steady when carried or when swayed; lifts head and shoulders in dorsal position as an effort toward sitting.

In locomotion movements the sequence in development is as follows:

One month—Makes crawling movements when laid prone on flat surface.

Nine months—Makes a locomotive reaction in prone position.

Ten months—Pulls self up to standing position.

Eleven months—Walks with help.

Twelve months—Stands alone; walks alone.

[5] GESELL, ARNOLD, "Infancy and Human Growth," pp. 17, 418, New York, The Macmillan Company, 1928.

Sitting posture develops according to this schedule with the average baby:

Four months—Sits with resistant body posture when supported by pillows.

Five months—Sits with slight prop.

Six months—Sits momentarily without support, if placed in favorable leaning position.

Eight months—Sits momentarily without support.

Nine months—Sits alone.

One of the tests under adaptive behavior is to present to the infant a wooden embroidery ring about 4½ inches in diameter painted bright red to which is attached a white string almost 10 inches long. This is the way a normal infant responds at different ages:

One month—Retains definite hold of the ring when it is placed in the hand.

Two months—Gives prolonged regard to dangling red ring.

Three months—Varied tactile manipulation of ring.

Four months—Closes in with both hands on dangling ring, when in dorsal position.

Seven months—Manipulates ring with sustained inspection.

Nine months—Uses string adaptively to pull ring.

If, instead of a ring, the child is offered one or more one-inch cubes he may be expected to respond somewhat as follows:

Four months—Regards one-inch cube on table.

Six months—Picks up cube from table on visual cue.

Seven months—Reaches persistently for remote cube.

Ten months—Accepts third cube or retains two cubes.

Twelve months—Secures cube wrapped in paper.

Thirteen months—Secures third cube; builds tower of two blocks.

F. Kuhlmann revised the Binet intelligence test extending it downwards to three months and during the past few

years F. L. Goodenough has been working on a revision of
the Kuhlmann test which will extend the age range as low
as eighteen months, and will be better standardized and
more reliable for prognosticating development. A test
somewhat similar in construction to the Kuhlmann has
been developed by Rachel Stutsman[6] at the Merrill-Palmer
School. The tests that make up this scale are largely
manipulation of concrete materials in various ways including such items as putting six round pegs and six square
pegs in holes in a board; putting sixteen cubes in a box;
fitting together a nest of four cubes; buttoning one, two,
and four buttons; building the Montessori little pink
tower; putting together the arms, legs, head, and body of a
cut-out manikin; copying a circle, cross, star. This test also
includes a limited amount of language through repetition
of words, answering questions, and responding to, "What
does the doggie say?" etc. One advantage of this scale is
that the same tests appear over and over again at various
age levels which gives an opportunity for comparing
children of different ages on the same performance. For
instance, children between thirty and thirty-five months
are given 170 seconds to button two buttons, but the time is
decreased for every six months until by sixty to sixty-five
months they are expected to complete the buttoning in
nineteen seconds. In most cases, however, such comparison
is on the basis of speed or time taken for completion rather
than on the increased difficulty of the performance.

However, these mental tests or developmental scales are
only in their beginnings. It is true that no great reliance
can yet be placed on intelligence quotients of children
during preschool years since more variation is found in the
mental rating of preschool children on various tests than is
found with older children. This is a fertile field for research,

[6] STUTSMAN, RACHEL, "Mental Measurement of Preschool Children," pp. x, 368,
Yonkers-on-Hudson, World Book Company, 1930.

and investigations of sequences in development should give fruitful results during the next decade.

Learning and Maturation.—It is necessary to know at what stage a child is in his development but it is also important to know the process by which he reached this stage. Is the child's increased ability due to learning or is it due to innate processes of growth? Was it maturity rather than learning? Which processes can we help by teaching and which come about as quickly without much effort on our part? One of the outstanding studies in the field of maturation and learning was made by Gesell and Thompson and is described in Chapter II of this book. Arthur T. Jersild and his associates of the Child Development Institute of Columbia University have this year undertaken some experiments with children from two to six years to see whether practice in certain performances really helps children.[7] Certain children were given practice for three months in tapping, in gripping and pulling, and in reproducing notes and musical intervals. Other children were matched with these children at the beginning but were given no practice during the three months. At the end of this period, the children who had been practicing did better than the other children in all performances. Another three months elapsed during which none of the children had any practice. When tests of tapping and pulling were then given, the children who had had no practice did substantially as well as those who had previously had practice. However, in tests of strength of grip the practiced children still maintained their advantage. The later tests on musical pitch and interval have not yet been given.

Another question which confronts us is that of the process by which children learn. What are the factors that influence a child's learning? Some interesting studies have

[7] JERSILD, ARTHUR T., and others, "The Relative Influence of Learning and Maturation in Young Children," 1931. Unpublished.

[14]

been made at Teachers College, Columbia University, and at the University of Iowa in the learning of children. In a study made by the author[8] of the ability of seventy-one children between four and six years of age to learn to recognize certain words, it was found that the arrangement of the amount of time between practice periods has an important effect upon how much children remember. No matter how much children of this age may over-learn a word on one day, some of them will not remember enough to recognize the word the next day. In no case, however, whether it was twenty-four hours or fourteen days later, was there total forgetting; something was saved each time which contributed to the relearning.

Julia A. Kirkwood[9] in a somewhat similar study of 203 children using blocks and pictures instead of words found that presentation of material on alternate days resulted in greater economy of learning than presentation on successive days. Even after the lapse of a year, she states that the children had retained something of their former learning.

There has been some discussion as to how children attack a problem situation. If a child is confronted with a problem does he attempt to solve it by trial and error or does he use insight? Wolfgang Koehler[10] made a series of studies with apes and found that the apes used trial and error but also insight. Augusta Alpert[11] tried similar problems with preschool children and found that children

---

[8] MEEK, LOIS HAYDEN, "A Study of Learning and Retention in Young Children," pp. ix, 96, New York, Teachers College, Columbia University, 1925.

[9] KIRKWOOD, JULIA A., "The Learning Process of Young Children," pp. 107, Iowa City, University of Iowa, 1926.

[10] KOEHLER, WOLFGANG, "The Mentality of Apes," pp. viii, 342, New York, Harcourt, Brace & Company, 1925.

[11] ALPERT, AUGUSTA, "The Solving of Problem-Situations by Preschool Children," pp. 69, New York, Bureau of Publications, Teachers College, Columbia University, 1928.

[15]

attack problems as apes do, usually by trial and error. However, no matter what the type of attack, according to Alpert, solution comes only if the child has gained insight into the situation. No solution was found to be caused directly by chance. On the basis of her study, Alpert recommends that learning situations should be made interesting but not too stimulating for young children; that it is wise to repeat once or twice a learning situation which a child has solved by insight; that self-conscious children will need help to focus their attention upon the problem rather than upon themselves or the adult; that children who lack confidence will need encouragement to try out all possible approaches to the problem; that children should be taught the habit of varying their solving procedure at a very early age; and that children should be encouraged to explore.

These recommendations emphasize, as you see, the influence of emotional adjustment on learning and the importance of mental hygiene in dealing with children. This point was also emphasized by the author in the study previously referred to. A special study of certain children who did not learn as readily as was expected indicated the following suggestions:

1. The necessity of organizing the learning situation so as to protect children from continued failure and dissatisfactions.

2. The need for teacher help and guidance at specific places in learning.

3. The need for thorough analysis of the learning situation to determine just when and what help and guidance should be given.

4. The need for a realization of the effect of emotional disturbances upon learning.

Social and Emotional Behavior.—The social development of children during the first six years of life is a rapid, intriguing process.[12] At birth an infant gives no evidence of differentiating people from the rest of his environment; he responds to them as he would to temperature, pressure, softness, presence of foods, etc. The newborn may smile but it is a reflex with no social implications.[13] However, during the second or third month he will smile in response to a smile from an adult or to clucking and baby talk of adults.[14] The amount of smiling increases steadily during the first year and seems to become gradually a method of social communication rather than just an expression of an emotional state. Laughing occurs later and does not change in its type during the early months.[15]

Buehler[16] through many hours of observations, has contributed much to our understanding of the social development of infants. In her infant tests she traces the development of social behavior thus:

Two months—Response to adult's glance.

Three months—Returning glance with smiling and cooing.

Four months—Expression of displeasure when adult stops playing with the child.

Five months—Reflecting friendly and angry facial expressions.

Six months—Actively seeking contact (turning point from passive to active social attitude).

Seven months—Distinguishes between angry and friendly facial expressions.

[12] A comprehensive and excellent discussion of the experimental studies in social development of preschool children will be found in: MURPHY, GARDNER and LOIS B. MURPHY, "Experimental Social Psychology," pp. 709, New York, Harper & Brothers, 1931.

[13] BLANTON, M. S., The Behavior of the Human Infant During the First Thirty Days of Life, *Psychological Review*, Vol. 24, pp. 456–483, 1917.

[14] JONES, MARY COVER, The Development of Early Behavior Patterns in Young Children, *Pedagogical Seminary and Journal of Genetic Psychology*, Vol. 33, No. 4, 1926.

[15] WASHBURN, R. W., A Study of the Smiling and Laughing of Infants in the First Year of Life, *Genetic Psychology Monographs*, Vol. 6, Nos. 5, 6, 1929.

[16] BUEHLER, *op. cit.*

Nine months—Becoming accustomed to strange adult.
Ten months—Turning in astonishment to an adult.
Eleven months—Organized play with adult.

This behavior is the reaction of children to adults. Buehler has also observed children's behavior toward one another during the first year. She finds that beginning at four and one-half months if two infants are placed near each other one child will look at the other, smile at the other child and cry if the other receives attention. Not until eight months will he offer a toy to the other child, coo to him, or imitate his movement. By nine and one-half months he will oppose the other child if he tries to take his toy and will also begin to play with him. More active interest comes about ten and one-half months when he will strive to get the other child's attention, will become ill-humored if the child moves away and will put aside his toy and turn to the other child.

The bringing together of children of preschool age into nursery school groups has afforded a rich opportunity for the study of the social behavior of young children. During the past five years some very interesting studies have been published. However, most of these studies deal with only small numbers of children and consequently we can draw general conclusions only tentatively, realizing that later studies may show that these traits or characteristics were peculiar to the group being studied. It has been found that the amount of time which children in the nursery school spend in groups varies with individual children but an average child will be a participant in two or three groups during a period of fifteen minutes.[17] The amount of social

[17] HUBBARD, RUTH M., A Method of Studying Spontaneous Group Formation, Chap. IV in "Some New Techniques for Studying Social Behavior," pp. 76-85, New York, Bureau of Publications, Teachers College, Columbia University, 1929. Child Development Monograph, No. 1.

participation increases with age, the younger children playing more often by themselves.[17,18] Twenty children between sixteen and thirty-two months who were studied by Ruth E. Arrington[19] spent the major proportion of their time while observed in the nursery school in active use of play materials. Social activity occurred only 5 per cent of the time and activities with themselves without other children or play materials about the same proportion of time. Talking to self occurred on an average of 8 per cent, laughing in 2 per cent, and crying in 1 per cent of the time. The social contacts made were more often verbal than of the physical type and were more frequently with children than with adults.

What these young children do when they are in groups is most interesting. Watching other children is a frequent activity. Children in the nursery school interfere with each other often but cooperate and imitate seldom. In a total of over 800 incidents of social relations among children E. A. Bott[20] found over 100 incidents of watching, 200 of interference, but only 70 of imitation and less than 50 of cooperation. Most of the contacts between nursery-school children are of a physical nature with a fairly definite tendency toward increase in the number of contacts from two years to four years.[18] Loomis also found evidence indicating that intentional physical contacts tended to decrease during the kindergarten period, from four years on. In general, as a child gets older, the physical contacts

[18] LOOMIS, ALICE MARIE, "A Technique for Observing the Social Behavior of Nursery School Children," pp. xi, 100, New York, Bureau of Publications, Teachers College, Columbia University, 1931. Child Development Monograph, No. 5.

[19] ARRINGTON, RUTH E., "Interrelations in the Behavior of Young Children," New York, Bureau of Publications, Teachers College, Columbia University, in press. Child Development Monograph.

[20] BOTT, E. A., and others, Observations and Training of the Fundamental Habits in Young Children, *Genetic Psychology Monographs*, No. 1, Vol. 4, pp. 5–158, July, 1928.

[19]

tend to become less representative of total social behavior and control of materials, gestures, and language take their place.

Age also seems to make a difference in other aspects of the social behavior of young children. Esther Van Cleve Berne[21] found that three- and four-year-old children exceed two-year-olds in interest in the group; in understanding their own property rights and in sociability, social conformance, responsibility for self and for others; but they also exceed in rivalry, jealousy, and criticism. The three-year-olds further exceeded the two-year-olds in independence of adults and in self-defense, while the four-year-olds exceeded both the two and three-year-olds in cooperation.

In just what way the intelligence of children affects their social behavior is not clear from the studies available. Hubbard found that children of similar mental ages tend to play together. She also found that the brighter children spent more time in groups while Loomis found that brighter children make more physical contacts. Berne found a relation between mental age and a large number of social traits such as participation, cooperation, responsibility for others, etc.

On the whole, at these early ages we have little evidence of differences between boys and girls in social behavior, but Berne found that girls of two, three, and four years exceeded boys in "motherliness" and that three-year-old boys exceeded three-year-old girls in irresponsibility for others.

Another factor which may have some effect on social behavior is muscular tension. In Loomis' study it was found that the higher the muscular tension of a child, the less tendency he showed to contacts with his associates.

---

[21] BERNE, ESTHER VAN CLEVE, "An Experimental Investigation of Social Behavior Patterns in Young Children," p. 93, Iowa City, University of Iowa, 1930.

The three children with the highest muscular tension definitely tended to limit their physical contacts with the other children. Such evidence, of course, does not justify any conclusions but indicates possibilities for further study.

All of the studies emphasize the differences which are found in individual children in social behavior. In some traits individual differences are more significant than age differences. Of course a very important thing for parents and teachers to know is whether these social traits shown so early in a child's behavior remain with him or whether they tend to disappear and change as time goes on. Two-year-olds and three-year-olds and four-year-olds in groups do show differences in behavior as previously discussed, especially in amount of social participation, number of physical contacts, understanding of property rights, social conformance, responsibility for self, etc. However, will children who are not average, who are different from the group at two or three, change as years go on or stay as they are? The answer is yet unknown, yet Loomis gives us a hint in her follow-up study of four children. She states that a child whose physical contacts at three years are so outstanding as to distinguish him from his associates on a purely statistical basis, may at a later age, with other children, show the same general behavior in aggressive participation in the group or in withdrawal or active friendly interaction in the group. She did find one child who had changed from withdrawing from the group to successful friendly resistance in the group after the lapse of a year.

Probably one of the most interesting studies which has been made of preschool children was Beaver's study of the gang.[22] We have always thought of gangs developing with

[22] BEAVER, ALMA PERRY, A Preliminary Report of a Study of a Preschool "Gang," Chap. VI in "Some New Techniques for Studying Social Behavior," pp. 99–117, New York, Bureau of Publications, Teachers College, Columbia University, 1929. Child Development Monograph, No. 1.

children around ten or eleven years of age but here is a gang of three three-year-old boys who played together regularly during their nursery-school year and continued to do so in the kindergarten. Roddie was three years and eight months old, Hendrick three years and six months, and Lionel three years and one month. Roddie, the oldest, initiated most of the contacts and they were directed at Lionel, the youngest. The most frequent combination was two rather than three boys. The other children in the nursery school used various methods to break into the group—persistence, ingenuity, and tact. But the gang was also fertile in methods of ousting the other children, varying from argument and verbal protest, to blows, shouting or screaming, pushing and ignoring.

Any adult who deals with preschool children as a parent, teacher, nurse, or psychologist, is concerned with the trait we call negativism or obstinancy or contrariness or stubborness. We have all probably had experience with a little child when he refused to do what was expected or did the exact opposite of what was expected or did something else. What causes such behavior? Do all children behave thus sometimes? Is there such a thing as the negativistic age? There have been a few experimental studies in this field and an extended amount of observation and discussion. Negativism seems to be a child's method of reacting when he is inhibited or interfered with. This interference may be physical, as is so often the case with infants, or it may be verbal through commands, rules, etc., during preschool years. Human beings seem doomed to interference. A baby from birth seems to be constantly struggling against the interferences, the inhibitions for which we are responsible. Bathing, clothing, lifting, carrying, holding—all interfere with a baby's activities. Gesell noted in his observations of a newborn that the baby cried every time he was moved or changed from one position to another

[22]

during the bathing and dressing episodes following birth. In a few months after birth, we begin to try to change a baby's habits of elimination. Dr. William White[23] believes this early interference with the fundamental pleasurable states occurring at urination and defecation is the primary cause of negativism, the degree of negativism depending upon the conditions under which these early habits are established. Reynolds[24] made an experimental study of 229 children between the ages of two years and five and a quarter years and concludes that the fundamental cause of negativism in preschool children is conflict between the wishes of the adult and the child. Refusals are made because the child has other interests. She emphasizes that negativism may be due to lack of adequate language expressions. For instance, "No!" for a two-year-old may mean many things, whereas a four-year-old would have a larger vocabulary to qualify his statement by such as "In a minute!" "When I'm through doing this!" Furthermore, a young child does not always understand the words he uses, sometimes saying, "I can't!" while he proceeds to do it or saying, "I'm not coming!" and then going immediately.

The types of activities which preschool children seem to refuse are those having to do with imitation of movements which call attention to themselves, and those requiring verbal responses. Reynolds found over a third of her children refusing to wave bye-bye and to clap their hands and about a third refusing to shake their heads. Rust[25]

[23] WHITE, WILLIAM A., "The Mental Hygiene of Childhood," pp. xv, 193, Boston, Little, Brown & Company, 1919.

[24] REYNOLDS, MARTHA MAY, "Negativism of Pre-School Children," New York, Bureau of Publications, Teachers College, Columbia University, pp. viii, 126. 1928.

[25] RUST, METTA MAUND, "The Effect of Resistance on Intelligence Test Scores of Young Children," New York, Bureau of Publications, Teachers College, Columbia University. Child Development Monograph, in press.

in studying resistance to a mental test by 100 three-year-olds found them resisting most often those tests that called for repetition of words, answers to questions, buttoning, imitation of movements, and discrimination of forms. In Nelson's study,[26] the tests most often refused were repetition of words, digits, or sentences and imitation of movement. She calls our attention to the fact, however, that sometimes children refused to do a test when the test was definitely above the mental age of the child.

This probably indicates the confusion which often exists in differentiating between resistant behavior as such and seemingly resistant behavior dictated by a child's insight into his own limitations and an unwillingness to subject himself to almost certain defeat.

Probably one of the most significant of personality traits is a child's method of meeting an interference or an inhibition. Of the three-year-old children who refused to do the tests in Rust's study, over 40 per cent were silent and another 25 per cent refused by saying something such as "No!" "I can't," "I don't know," "I don't want to say that." Others made remarks related to something in the room, suggesting doing something else, suggesting a delay, asking questions, making irrelevant remarks, suggesting the removal or destroying of the test, asking for help. A few children tried to get away or out of the room, used the material in a different way, pushed material away, went after other material, or tried to destroy material. Children of preschool age are sometimes quite fertile in thinking up excuses for their failures. In one experiment[27] where children were asked to open a box that was

[26] NELSON, JANET FOWLER, "Personality and Intelligence," pp. 62, New York, Bureau of Publications, Teachers College, Columbia University, 1931. Child Development Monograph, No. 4.
[27] MARSTON, LESLIE R., "The Emotions of Young Children," pp. 99, Iowa City, University of Iowa, 1925.

too difficult for them, one boy said, "Guess it's sweaty like I am!" and "I guess it's tired and wants to rest!" A girl remarked, "I fell down and hurt my two knees and one thumb, so I couldn't open it!" And another boy repeatedly explained that it was "too hard" on his sore finger though the psychologist could see no symptoms of a sore on the finger which was shown to him.

One interesting question which arises in studying children is the interrelations of various personality traits. Do children that laugh a great deal also cry a great deal, or does laughing go with joyousness, activity, and getting along with one's fellows, while crying goes with despondency, inactivity, resistance, and conflicts with others? The answer to this has not been found but several studies are interesting. In one study[28] a slight relationship was found between physical activity and leadership, sociality, extroversion, attractiveness of personality, and frequency of laughter. There was also a slight relation between the degree of physical activity of a child and the likelihood of his becoming a behavior problem. It was also found that the children who talk most are very likely to be extroverts, to lead other children, and to play with others.

A few studies have been made which show that children very early begin to display tendencies toward a distinct personality type. Washburn[29] for instance, in studying the smiling and laughing of infants during the first year states that her children could be classified into three groups: those who ranked high in smiling and laughing and low in crying or sober behavior; those who smiled and laughed about as much as they cried or were sober; and those who ranked high in crying and sober behavior. These babies

---

[28] GOODENOUGH, F. L., Inter-relationships in the Behavior of Young Children, *Child Development*, Vol. 1, pp. 29–48, 1930.

[29] WASHBURN, *op. cit.*

were very consistent in the way they behaved from observation to observation, most of them keeping their characteristic response after a year.

Some studies seem to indicate a tendency also for children during the preschool years to be rather distinct personality types in regard to so-called extroversion and introversion. These words are used to describe on the one hand the individual who displays in his social contacts an outward movement of interest toward the object (extroversion) or on the other hand a movement of interest away from the object toward the subject (introversion). Marston[30] developed a rating scale which attempted to distinguish how a child rated on such traits as self-consciousness, vocal expression, group activities, sensitiveness to others' opinions, sociability, response to another's wishes, confidence, attitude toward strangers, secretiveness, modesty, energy, judgment, responsiveness to environment, speed of movement, shifting in activities, and emotional expression. He also undertook some experiments to measure: social resistance, compliance with another's will, caution in making decisions, interest in environment, self-assertion. The 100 children he studied were between the ages of two and six years. Even as young as this, he found them divided into introverts, extroverts, and ambiverts (those who combined traits of both extreme groups). The fourth group which we might expect to find, namely the balanced type whose traits seem to follow pretty generally a medium line, was absent in these particular children. Whether this would be true if a large number of unselected children were studied, we do not know.

Play Materials.—Observations of children in nursery schools and in progressive kindergartens have given us informal information about play activities and play materials which has influenced greatly the toys and play

[30] MARSTON, *op. cit.*

equipment available for young children. From the kindergarten has come a series of books under the editorship of Professor Patty Smith Hill of Columbia University.[31] Much of the nursery school literature has discussed play materials and play activities of children. Especially noteworthy is "Children in the Nursery School" by Harriet Johnson. Emphasis has been placed on large equipment for climbing, sliding, swinging, push and pull toys for two- and three-year-olds, manipulative materials for block building, sawing, hammering, etc. However, very little experimental work has been done either by psychologists or educators. Probably the best information which we have has come from the observations which have been made on groups of children in the nursery school or kindergarten during the morning play period.[32]

Hulson[33] observed children's use of playthings in the nursery school and kindergarten and ranked the material used under four headings which showed how often each piece of material was chosen, how long the children spent with each, how persistent the material was in the child's interest, and whether the material aided social play or individual play. When she rated the twenty odd play materials on these characteristics, *blocks* were ranked first; *sand* and *watching* were respectively second and third in all but social value; *house corner*

[31] See Childhood Education Series of books published by Scribner's, New York, including such books as the following:

THORNE, ALICE G., "Music for Young Children," pp. xix, 158, 1929.

GARRISON, CHARLOTTE GANO, "Permanent Play Materials for Young Children," pp. xxii, 122, 1926.

[32] A comprehensive survey of thirty-four studies on the play and occupational interests of preschool children has recently been made by Christine Heinig of the Child Development Institute, Teachers College, Columbia University. The studies reported in this section were taken from Miss Heinig's unpublished manuscript.

[33] Hulson, EVA LEAH, "An Analysis of the Free Play of Four-Year-Old Children through Consecutive Studies of Individuals," Iowa City, University of Iowa, 1928. Unpublished.

fourth and *children* sixth in times chosen and minutes spent; *kiddy-car* fifth in all but persistence; and *crayon and paper* seventh in number of minutes used and social value.

. Bott[34] in a study of 12 children, two to four and one-half years old found that they preferred materials in this order: raw materials (beans, blocks, cubes, etc.), locomotive materials (trains, tricycle, wagon, etc.), pattern materials (beads, puzzles, etc.), and mechanical materials. Another study of three-year-old children[35] showed that cylinders, blocks, and color pairs were the preferred playthings. Van Alstyne's recent study[36] of 112 children from two to five years showed that out of 25 play materials, children preferred clay, doll corner, easel painting, assorted sizes of floor blocks, blocks that lock, hollow blocks, wagons, dishes, dolls, small cars, scissors, crayons, and color cubes. With the two- and three-year-olds, clay and doll corner held first place whereas the four- and five-year-olds chose blocks first, with clay and crayons also high favorites. Heinig concludes from her survey that children seem to prefer raw materials (such as blocks, clay, paints, etc.) with blocks as the favorite for all preschool ages; two-year-olds are the only group who seem much interested in mechanical toys; clay is popular with all children; dolls and doll corner are especially popular with girls; beads are seldom chosen.

Language.—Much of the mental and social growth of children depends upon learning methods of communica-

[34] BOTT, HELEN, Observation of Play Activities in Nursery Schools, *Genetic Psychology Monographs*, No. 4, Vol. 4, No. 1, pp. 44–48, July, 1928.

[35] BRIDGES, K. M. BANHAM, Occupational Interests of Three Year Old Children, *Pedagogical Seminary*, Vol. 4, pp. 415–423, September, 1927.

[36] VAN ALSTYNE, DOROTHY, "A Study of the Differences of Play Behavior of Children of Two, Three, Four and Five Years," unpublished study done at Garden Apartments, Franklin, and Winnetka Public Nursery Schools, under auspices of the Behavior Research Fund, Chicago, 1931.

tion. At birth this is almost entirely confined to crying, grimacing, stiffening of muscles, and similar behavior. Gradually the child learns through these six years to understand the language, facial expressions, gestures, and movements of those about him and to make known his own needs and desires to others by similar means. These observable changes in behavior appear gradually during the first two years, and then develop by leaps and bounds. According to Blanton[37] during the first month, although there are differentiated cries, no one cry is used for any particular situation. But by four months of age, Gesell[38] found that from 65 to 81 per cent of children can vocalize two or more distinguishable sounds. The first year is a year of sound experimentation; individual investigators find children from four months to twelve months making all the sounds in the language. Children begin to talk from nine months on. Nice[39] states that at one year a great many children have not begun to talk while at eighteen months some have not. Studies of individual children at twelve months show a variation in vocabulary of from 1 to 24 words with an average of 7. At two years of age there is wide variation of from 5 to 1212 words with an average of 328 words.[40] Another study of 25 children gives an average of 272 words. The most usual estimate for two years is from 200 to 300 words. By three years of age this has increased to an approximate average of 900; at four, 1500 words; at five, 2000 words and at six, 2500 words.[41]

[37] BLANTON, *op. cit.*

[38] GESELL, "The Mental Growth of the Pre-School Child."

[39] NICE, M. M., On the Size of Vocabularies, *American Speech*, Vol. 2, pp. 1-7, 1926-1927.

[40] Compiled by M. M. Nice from 47 individual vocabularies.

[41] These are round numbers taken from Smith, M. E., "An Investigation of the Development of the Sentence and the Extent of Vocabulary in Young Children," pp. 92, Iowa City, University of Iowa, 1926.

It must be remembered that the ability to use language is determined not only by increase in vocabulary but by sentence formation, parts of speech and fluency. There is a steady growth during the preschool years, in all aspects of language development. McCarthy's study[42] of 50 consecutive verbal responses of 140 children from eighteen to fifty-four months of age gives a remarkable picture of the speed of language development. She states:

The child at eighteen months of age knows only a few single words, yet in a short time—three years—he has acquired several thousand words, which he is able to combine into sentences as long and as complex as the adult uses in his everyday conversation; he has a ready command of all the inflections of the language and can use language for communicating all his thoughts, needs and desires.

This study also indicated a more rapid development of language among girls.

Van Alstyne[43] made an investigation of environmental factors influencing the vocabulary of three-year-old children. She lists the following fifteen factors:

1. Suitable play materials and books.
2. Conversation with child by adults.
3. Proper physical surroundings and routine.
4. Other children in the home.
5. Association with other children.
6. Good economic conditions.
7. Suitable excursions.
8. Social atmosphere in the home, visits to others, etc.
9. Responsibility for certain personal and household tasks.
10. Reading to the child.

[42] McCarthy, Dorothea A., "The Language Development of the Preschool Child," pp. xiii, 174, Minneapolis, University of Minnesota Press, 1930.

[43] Van Alstyne, Dorothy, "The Environment of Three-year-old Children," pp. vii, 108, New York, Bureau of Publications, Teachers College, Columbia University, 1929.

11. Parent's use of good English.
12. Educational status of parents.
13. Stimulation to independent activity.
14. Interest of parents in the child's activity.
15. Knowledge of level reached by the child and interest in his reaching the next state.

Other factors which seem to influence language development are intelligence and the social background of parents.[44] Scientific studies are lacking but experience seems to emphasize that the speech of children will be retarded if children are neglected or not talked to (as in orphan asylums and institutions) or are so waited on that there is no need for language, or are unusually shy, fearful, or emotionally unstable. Problems in language also arise sometimes with children of parents speaking a foreign language. Retardation in language behavior has been found to be closely allied to many other personality adjustment problems.

Conclusion

Such a brief survey can only give a kaleidoscopic picture of the rapidly increasing information concerning the psychological development of preschool children. Among the important phases which I have found it necessary to omit completely in this short sketch are the group of studies and the accumulating information concerning the psychological aspects of the establishment of the fundamental habits of eating, sleeping, and eliminating.[45] Nor have the topics which I have chosen for discussion been

[44] A more complete discussion of language development on the basis of research studies will be found in *28th Yearbook of the National Society for the Study of Education*, Part II, Chap. III., pp. x, 875, Bloomington, Illinois, Public Schools Publishing Company, 1928.

[45] An excellent discussion of these habits by Dr. Helen Thompson Woolley has recently been published in "Handbook of Child Psychology," edited by Murchinson, published by Clark University Press.

treated exhaustively since an extended presentation of all of the research studies and of the psychological information available on preschool children would far exceed the confines of a single chapter. If this brief presentation, therefore, can be considered an introduction to the subject, the reader will be well repaid for following up this slight acquaintanceship with the more intimate associations afforded in current literature.

Chapter II

THE STUDY AND GUIDANCE OF INFANT BEHAVIOR

by ARNOLD GESELL

IN the study of infant behavior it is natural that we should call to our aid the cinematic camera. Cinematography, which combines in a remarkable manner the principles of optics, mechanics, and chemistry, is both a product and an instrument of modern science. We need such a powerful instrument for the exploration of the bewildering and almost kaleidescopic eventfulness of human infancy.[1]

The cinema cannot immediately solve some of the more metaphysical problems of the infant's psychology—the deep and hidden essence of his notions of time and space, his satisfactions and sufferings, his appetites, attitudes and Weltanschauung! There is still a veil which neither the intuitive eye of man nor the actinic eye of the camera can pierce. But why lament the present unknowable when there are such vast stretches of uncharted visible psychology?

The cinema can capture the visible behavior of the infant. The motion-picture film is a succession of individual photo-

[1] A sound film entitled "The Study of Infant Behavior" has recently been made with the cooperation of Electrical Research Products, Inc., of the Western Electric Company, New York. This film portrays the work of The Yale Psycho-Clinic, and carries a synchronized spoken explanatory comment. It pictures the developmental examination procedures, the operation of the photographic dome, methods for the study of cinema records, the one-way-vision screen and the activities of the guidance nursery. Special emphasis is given to the photographic techniques which have been developed in the laboratory of the clinic for the motion-picture investigation of the growth of early human behavior.

[33]

graphs or frames—in the 16-millimeter size about forty per linear foot, a thousand per durational minute. Each frame constitutes a comprehensive record of a moment of behavior. A thousand frames depict a thousand moments. So authentic are these serial instantaneous records that when they are projected in their original sequence, the behavior itself is literally restored. The infant is resurrected on the screen.

It is a paradoxical form of embalming. For although the behavior characteristics are permanently preserved in chemical emulsion, they come again to life. Meanwhile, the infant himself is in no way deprived of his further growth! In a month or two he acquires new characteristics of behavior, which obscure his recent immaturity; but in the film the past survives, free from the improvements of later development. It is obvious that such graphic reanimating records of the reacting infant can assist us to a scientific understanding of behavior mechanics and to a charting of the course of behavior development. Let us illustrate.

Beginning as early as sixteen weeks we place an infant in a diminutive chair (of the Morris type) with a supportive band. For convenience and orderliness of observation this chair rests on the platform of a clinical crib at a height of thirty inches. The crib has adjustable side rails, which support a table top on a level with the infant's elbows. This table top presently becomes the stage for the observation of the infant's characteristic behavior. We place a selected object on the table to determine his responses. Even before a stimulating object is in position the infant reacts to the table top itself. In his psychology the table surface becomes a stimulating object and it always remains a factor in the total behavior picture.

We now place upon the table a sugar pellet 7 millimeters in diameter. The pellet is within the infant's arm length.

He is sixteen weeks, or four lunar months of age. He fixates upon the examiner's hand as the pellet is placed in position. Rarely he fixates upon the pellet. At twenty weeks he may regard the pellet and advance upon it with crude inward approach of one or both hands. At twenty-four weeks he scratches with pronate paw-like hand in the vicinity of the pellet. At twenty-eight weeks he may rake it up with simultaneous flexion of the fingers against the palm. At thirty-two weeks the thumb and forefinger begin to display a preeminence in the prehensory act. This preeminence becomes progressively perfected so that at forty weeks the infant plucks the pellet with pincer-like utilization of the index finger and thumb. At fifty-two weeks he plucks the pellet yet more adeptly and may deposit it in the mouth of a bottle, though his own mouth remains a strongly competing destination.

The tiny pellet serves as well as a more technical device to illustrate some of the problems of developmental psychology. Behavior grows. Every lunar month witnesses distinguishable changes in the patterning of the behavior manifestations. Though the stimulus object is a tiny one it evidently evokes the whole organism, as the puck on ice enlists the concentrating hockey player. The reactions to the pellet involve the infant's total body posture, his legs, his arms, his head station, the posturing of his facial muscles, the posturing of his forearm, wrist, thumb, and fingers. These reactions are not discrete units in loose aggregation. They are dynamically correlated with respect to timing, spacing, and direction. It is such inner correlation which organizes behavior and imparts configuration to its expressions; be it posture, locomotion, prehension, eye movements, adaptive behavior, or even social behavior

The chief interest and the significance of infant behavior lie in phenomena of change, or emergence, increment, and decrement. The infant himself alters so rapidly and

[35]

so diversely that it.is difficult to make many generalizations about him. We cannot even take a week to make a thoroughgoing investigation of an individual infant, because by the time the week is over the infant we began to investigate has changed into a being so different from an experimental standpoint he is no longer the selfsame subject.[2]

So swift and continuous are these changes that in the first six years of life the individual traverses far more development ground than he will ever again compass in a similar period. If there were some volumetric unit for expressing the quantity or current flow of development from birth to the age of twenty-four years, we should find the resultant graph rising with a rocketing sweep in the preschool years. If there were some graphic method for expressing the multiplicity and the variety of behavior patterns, the diagram would show a widely disproportionate range of behavior in the period of infancy. When the wealth of behavior equipment acquired in the prenatal period is cast into the reckoning, the enormous concentration of development in early life becomes yet more striking.

The newborn babe is almost a pulp from the standpoint of postural control; at two years he can run; by six years he may be acquiring the rudiments of golf or musical skill. In the field of perception he advances from a stage of sketchy, wavering, ocular responses to fine discriminations of color, size, form. At birth he reflexively clasps a rod (or crayon) with eyes crudely wandering or vacantly transfixed; at six he adaptively scans the perimeter of a square or a triangle, reproducing each form with self-directed crayon. The birth cry, scant in modulation and social meaning, marks the low level of language, which

[2] For a more extended discussion of the relationship between age and behavior development, see "The Foundations of Experimental Psychology," Chap. XVI, Worcester, Mass., Clark University Press, 1929; also Gesell's "Infancy and Human Growth," New York, The Macmillan Company, 1928.

in two years rises to sentence structure, and in six years to elaborated syntactic speech, with evidences of primitive ideas of causality. In personality make-up there is enormous progress; the school beginner is already so highly organized (both socially and biologically) that he definitely foreshadows the sort of individual he will be in mature years.

The task of developmental psychology is to give systematic formulation to this prodigious complex of early behavior growth. In spite of its inexhaustible complexity and variability, the developmental stream of early human behavior assumes ordered pattern. If there were no evidence of underlying, lawful design, scientific study of infant behavior would scarcely be possible.

Pattern is a protean word, but it is useful; it is valid. In the quantitative and comparative study of behavior pattern lies a solid pathway to infant psychology. In a biological sense the infant mind is as real and almost as tangible as the body with which it is associated; for the infant mind manifests itself in a developing system of patterns. In terms of pattern, the infant mind has as much structure, as much form, as much direction and design, as much growth and stability as the body. Indeed one of the most impressive facts in regard to the human infant is the stability and durability of his mental organization in the face of unfavorable environment and of physical adversity. A mind with such organic integrity will yield to biometric study and ultimately to laws of prediction and control.

Prediction and control—these are rather ambitious concepts in the light of our meager knowledge of the laws of human behavior, but they are permissible as scientific goals. Oliver Wendell Holmes in his biography of Ralph Waldo Emerson (1885) has an interesting paragraph which bears quotation in this connection.

But certainly no physiologist, no cattle breeder, [says Holmes] no Calvinistic predestinarian could put his view more vigorously than Emerson, who dearly loves a picturesque statement, has given it in these words which have a dash of science, a flash of imagination, and a hint of the delicate wit that is one of his characteristics: *People are born with the moral or with the material bias: —uterine brothers with this diverging destination: and I suppose with high magnifiers Mr. Fraunhofer or Dr. Carpenter might come to distinguish in the embryo at the fourth day, this is a whig and that a free soiler* . . .

Emerson's picturesque statement brings us to a brief consideration of the useful applications of psychology in the guidance of infant behavior. The psychology of infancy is itself in a stage of infancy and not yet competent to cast a horoscope for the newborn babe. But every decade witnesses some progress in scientific knowledge which gives us a little deeper insight into the controlling factors of human behavior.

Modern science has already profoundly changed our outlook upon infant behavior. The outlook of earlier generations was colored by authoritarian, pietist, romantic, and theological concepts which are disappearing under the rationalizing influence of biological thought. This trend toward a new rationalism has gathered great strength in the present century. Recent scientific developments in child psychology have contributed a heavy share toward the transformation of temper in the attitudes assumed by the old toward the young.

The change in the climate of adult opinion is leading to more impersonal, less sentimental but more sympathetic parent-child relationships. The increase in sympathy is the result of better understanding. There is a more just appreciation of the meaning of immaturity and of individual differences, particularly with respect to children of school age.

[38]

It is still popularly believed, however, that infants are to a considerable extent alike; and there is accordingly a strong tendency to treat them much alike. Individualized educational guidance of infants remains in a very rudimentary stage. Methods for the measurement of individual differences in infancy must be extended so that we may reckon with these differences at the beginning of the child's life cycle. Here lies one of the useful fields of application for developmental psychology. In the infant, mind and body, health and disease, education and hygiene are in intimate interrelation. It therefore seems probable that methods of psychological measurement will be applied in close alliance with biological and medical methods of developmental supervision.

Consecutive studies of infants show that individual differences in capacity, emotional characteristics, personality traits, and body type declare themselves early. These differences are comparable in kind and degree to those observed in later life. Many of the differences are due to innate or constitutional factors and are not the direct result of experience or conditioning. The extreme views of behaviorism with regard to infant conditioning are not borne out by experimental observation of individual infants and of identical twins.

The guidance of infant behavior should be governed by a careful regard for the intrinsic limitations of the infant's organism as well as the plasticity of that organism. The areas, the modes, the incidence, and hygiene of conditioning are themselves conditioned by factors of growth and of individual equipment.

The relations between learning and growth are interestingly suggested in the developmental similarities and divergences of twins. A brief reference to a study[3] reported

[3] GESELL, ARNOLD, and HELEN THOMPSON, Learning and Growth in Identical Infant Twins: An Experimental Study by the Method of Co-Twin Control,

at greater length elsewhere will serve to suggest some of these relations which concern the educational psychology of the rapidly growing infant.

The subjects were a pair of highly identical twins observed from early infancy. At the age of forty-six weeks, when repeated measurements had established the thorough-going mental and physical similarity of the twins, it was decided to determine the influence of training confined to one twin, by using an experimental method which we may designate as the method of co-twin control. T became the trained twin; C was reserved as a control.

Accordingly, Twin T was systematically trained for twenty minutes daily over a period of six weeks, in two fields of behavior—stair climbing and cube behavior, including prehension, manipulation, and constructive play with a dozen 1-inch red cubes. An experimental staircase arrangement of five treads was used and for ten minutes daily Twin T was put through her paces. At forty-eight weeks she scaled the stairs for the first time with slight assistance. At the conclusion of the six weeks' training period (age, one year) she was a relatively expert climber. At that age her untrained co-twin C would not yet scale the staircase, even with assistance. At the age of fifty-three weeks, however, when C was again confronted with the staircase she climbed to the top without any assistance and without any previous specific training whatsoever. In these circumstances the form and the efficiency of her pattern of climbing were almost purely a function of the maturation of the appropriate neural counterparts.

Twin C was then given an experimental course of training in stair climbing, two weeks in length. At the end of this

Genetic Psychology Monographs, Vol. 6, No. 1, pp. 1–123, July, 1929. See also "The Foundations of Experimental Psychology," Chap. 16, The Individual in Infancy, pp. 628–660, Worcester, Mass., Clark University Press, 1929.

period (age, fifty-five weeks) she approached Twin T in climbing skill. By means of the motion picture it was possible to make a comparison of the climbing ability of C at fifty-five weeks (after two weeks of training) with that of T at fifty-two weeks (after six weeks of training). This comparison introduced an interesting form of relativity into the investigation and brought out the significant fact that, although T had been trained three times longer and seven weeks earlier, this advantage was more than overcome by the three weeks of C's added age. Again the powerful influence of maturation on infant behavior patterns is made clear. Early training altered slightly the form of the pattern and hastened the acquisition of facility, but left no considerable or decisive locomotor advantage in favor of Twin T.

In the field of cube play the experiment clearly showed that training had no significant effects upon the patterns of prehension, manipulation, and constructive exploitation. Although Twin C had enjoyed no special opportunities in the handling of cubes, her cube behavior was fully equal to that of T after a six weeks' training period. The similarity in the temporal and spatial details of the patterns was confirmed in this case by a time-space analysis of the cinema record of these behavior patterns. This does not, however, mean that there were no changes in the patterns of cube behavior during the training period from forty-six to fifty-two weeks. On the contrary, the records, when analyzed, show consistent and incontrovertible weekly increments. Indeed, a day-by-day analysis of the diurnal records of cube behavior suggested the presence of daily increments, or at least a relatively continuous drift toward progressive changes in the cube performance patterns. These changes when viewed over daily intervals appeared as though achieved by steady processes of developmental decrement and increment rather than by a saltatory or

[41]

zigzag course. Spurts and plateaus were not conspicuous, but at this stage of the life cycle there was a relatively constant trend toward daily change.

This progressive daily changing apparently occurs by a process of continuous emergence which tends to lift the level of development slowly and steadily as though by tide action rather than by rhythmic spurt. We would explain the resistance of the patterns of cube behavior to the influence of training and conditioning by the fact that these patterns are basically under the stress and regulation of the intrinsic organic factors of maturation. The very fact that there is a growth trend toward daily change of pattern makes the behavior less susceptible to stereotypy and conditioning.

It may be argued that such limitations of learning apply only to locomotion and manual behavior, but not to such socialized functions as language. But even in the sphere of language, the developmental mechanism of maturation asserts itself. In a revealing experimental study by Lois Curry Strayer[4] made with the very twins under discussion, the significance of maturity factors was demonstrated. Using again the method of co-twin control she compared the relative efficacy of early and deferred vocabulary training. Twin T's training was begun at eighty-four weeks and continued through eighty-eight weeks of age. Twin C, reserved as a control, was trained in an identical manner from eighty-nine weeks through ninety-two weeks of age. The observations were made with great care and detail on a 24-hour basis for each of the consecutive sixty-three days of the entire study.

The detailed results were treated quantitatively and proved decisive with reference to the issue. "Not only was

[4] STRAYER, LOIS CURRY, Language and Growth. The Relative Efficacy of Early and Deferred Language Training Studied by the Method of Co-Twin Control, *Genetic Psychology Monographs*, Vol. 8, No. 3, pp. 209–319, September, 1930.

training which was begun with a maturational advantage of five weeks more effective than earlier training, but the pattern of response was more mature." Twin *C*, though she embarked on her vocabulary training five weeks later than her co-twin, gained, if anything, thereby. She showed fewer infantilisms, did not need as many repetitions to learn, did not double syllables as often (as *ba-ba* for ball), was freer from interference of association, incorporated new words more quickly into her spontaneous jargon, and extended her applications earlier, more widely, and more frequently. These latter tendencies, in particular, being relatively independent of training bespoke the influence of maturational level.

These studies of twins concern the mechanisms of behavior development. It would be hazardous to expand the specific findings into sweeping generalizations, minimizing the power of educational influences. The tongue which a child speaks derives from his environment. The vernacular can scarcely be sought in his genes. And many subtle inflections of his characteristic conversations as a man, will trace genetically and dynamically to the history of his personality.

So complex is the social life of the human infant of today that we may concede him in one breath generous capacities of learning as well as of indigenous growth. The dynamic sensitiveness of his personality organization to his milieu is incontestable. But we risk injustice to the infant by over-stressing his plasticity and conditionability. He grows in accordance with endowment as well as environment. Training cannot transcend maturation, but must respect it. Slowly the biological sciences will define the safeguards, the scope, the nature and needs of growth potencies in infancy. And in time the guidance of infant behavior will rest on more scientific foundation.

[43]

Chapter III

PSYCHOLOGY AND EDUCATION

by ARTHUR I. GATES

PSYCHOLOGY has probably been applied to the theories and practices of education more extensively than to any other professional field. It now forms the basis of the curriculum in nearly all progressive schools of education. There are, indeed, few facts or principles of psychology which may not be usefully applied to education, and few problems in education which may be solved without a consideration of the facts of psychology.

In the space at my disposal in this volume, I can suggest but a few of the many practical uses which education is now making of psychology. Instead of discussing the abstract principles of psychology, I shall describe concretely a few educational results or practices which have grown directly from psychological research. I shall give an illustration, first, of an instance in which psychology has added greatly to our understanding of a basal school skill; second, two case studies to indicate the character of the diagnosis of educational difficulties; third, a suggestion of the influence of psychology in reforming the school curriculum; fourth, an illustration of a modern method of teaching; and, fifth, a few comments concerning the possibilities and the economic and social significance of adult education.

Applications of the Results of Investigations of Reading

Many educational reforms effected during the past twenty-five years find their origin in the researches conducted in psychological laboratories soon after their establishment. Indeed, some of the most significant contributions to education developed directly from the first investigations made by one of our best-known American psychologists, Dr. J. McKeen Cattell.

Working in the first psychological laboratory in Leipzig, under Wundt, Dr. Cattell in one investigation published in 1885 inaugurated two lines of study that have been most actively pursued. When he first pointed out the psychological significance of individual differences in reading, reaction time, and other mental activities, he initiated the movement which has developed into the present elaborate science and practice of mental measurement. No other phase of the scientific study of education has attracted so many workers and developed so far as a professional field as that of tests and measurements. The second line of inquiry inaugurated by Cattell's initial studies, sprang from his discovery of the fact that a literate person can recognize many whole words in less time than he can perceive a single letter. He found, in fact, that in reading, a person does not perceive individual letters or syllables as such, but a whole word or several words as a unit. This discovery, suggesting as it did the fallacy in the older notion that the child should be taught letters and phonograms as a means of learning to recognize words, initiated the psychological researches which have resulted in a complete revolution in our methods of teaching children to read. Children now learn from the start to recognize whole words organized in meaningful sentences.

Since most of us were taught to read before the improvements suggested by Dr. Cattell's study were put into effect —the fact is that they have been widely incorporated in methods of instruction only recently—some of us may be suffering from limitations due to the older methods. It is not difficult to diagnose one's own case. First, you

[45]

should determine the rate at which you normally read silently, with full understanding, material of about the level of complexity found in a good magazine article. Tests upon groups of graduate students varying in age from twenty-five to fifty show that the average rate of silent reading of such material by well-educated adults is about 250 words per minute. You can compare your rate with this figure. However, a considerable number of such adults, about 12 to 18 per cent, read only 165 or fewer words per minute. The average rate at which people ordinarily speak in discourse is about 160 words per minute. Hence, from 12 to 18 per cent of the adults who spend a large part of their time in reading fail to exceed the rate of speech. This limitation is usually due to the analytic, oral reading drill which was formerly used in teaching and which, as a result of the studies initiated by Dr. Cattell, has since been abolished in progressive schools.

At the present time, any child of average intelligence is expected, before he reaches the end of the sixth grade, to be able to read silently at twice the rate of speaking. What is more important, many adults, despite their long habituation to the old, inadequate methods, can and do greatly increase their speed of reading. In fact, they are often able to double it after a few weeks of re-training. As a conservative estimate, it may be said that if every literate American over fifteen years of age who spends two hours or more a day in reading could be given such training for a month, the saving in time required to do the nation's workaday reading, valued at fifty cents an hour, would amount to more than five billion dollars a year.

The Diagnosis of Difficulties in the Basal School Skills

Reading is probably the most complex and subtle of the scholastic skills. Failures in reading were, until recently, more frequent than failures in any other subject. They are also more serious in their consequence. Over 90 per cent of the failures to earn promotion, in general, in the first three grades are due to difficulties in reading. Unless a child can read fairly well, he can do little of the work above the third grade. A crucial problem in most schools, consequently, is that of diagnosing and remedying deficiencies or disabilities in reading.

The methods used in diagnosing difficulties in reading are similar in many respects to those employed in the practice of medicine in diagnosing physical disorders. In a well-equipped reading laboratory, materials and instruments are found for forty or more separate tests and observations. As in the field of medicine, the number and type of tests employed will vary from case to case. To give some idea of the technique, I shall briefly outline the diagnosis of a particular case.

This is the case of a boy, to whom we shall give the fictitious name of John, who had been unable to learn to read after spending two and a half years in school. During this time various methods of teaching reading had been employed without success. John was finally considered to be an unteachable case so far as reading was concerned. He had, in fact, been diagnosed as a case of "congenital word-blindness," a term frequently used to designate the most extreme form of native inaptitude for reading or spelling or both.

When John was brought in for diagnosis he was eight and a half years old. He was then trying to do the work of the second grade, much of it unsuccessfully, due to his inability to read. John was first given a series of standardized tests in reading ability. The tests here used were identical with those widely employed in public schools for measuring the attainments of pupils in different aspects of reading skill. The tests showed objectively what the teachers had reported, namely, that John was incapable of

[47]

reading with understanding even simple material of the type found in first-grade books.

The next test given to John was the Stanford Revision of the Binet Test for general intelligence. This is the instrument used extensively in progressive schools for the purpose of appraising a child's general ability to acquire such scholastic abilities as those for reading, arithmetic, spelling, and the like. The test is designed to show the degree to which the child has native capacities for learning scholastic subjects. As a matter of fact, difficulties in learning to read are more frequently due to low intelligence than to any other single cause. In a modern public school those pupils whose intelligence quotients are 70 per cent or less, roughly speaking, of the normal or average degree of intelligence, are grouped together in "special" or "opportunity" classes. In these classes reading is taught by special methods adapted to those of limited aptitude and slow growth in reading ability. John, however, earned on the intelligence test an intelligence quotient of 116. This means that the boy had general intellectual ability of a superior sort; in fact, it exceeded the quotient of average children by approximately 16 per cent. This finding made it clear that John's difficulty in reading could not be attributed to dullness or intellectual retardation. If John's equipment otherwise and the character of his teaching had been as good as the average, he should have exceeded the average child in his reading ability.

In a similar manner an examination was made of all the other native capacities or constitutional factors which are involved in learning to read, since a deficiency in any one capacity might be responsible for difficulty in acquiring reading ability. For example, since defective vision of certain types may seriously interfere with the processes of perception required in reading, a series of tests of visual acuity were given. It was found, however, that John's general vision was normal. Further tests to diagnose his ability to perceive small visual figures, of which the printed word is one type, showed that his perceptual capacities were above the average in dealing with almost every type of visual figure with the exception of English words. Hence his difficulty in reading could not be attributed to any constitutional slowness or incapacity in discriminating between small visual figures.

The next series of tests dealt with hearing and auditory discrimination. It was found that John's hearing was normal and that he showed no limitation in distinguishing word-like sounds from each other. Hence there was no evidence of any constitutional deficiency in the field of hearing and auditory perception.

A number of tests were then utilized to measure what is often called the "memory span," or "immediate memory" for visual items. Since children are occasionally found who can perceive visual figures rather well but who cannot keep them in mind, tests of the visual memory span are of value. In the case of John, however, no deficiency in these respects was found. The same conclusions were reached for his auditory memory span, after a series of tests for immediate memory of letters, nonsense words, numbers, and sounds had been given.

Tests were then tried which are designed to measure what may be called associative capacities. Reading involves not only the accurate perception and memory of the printed configurations, but also the capacity to connect or associate these configurations with meanings or with other reactions, such as those of speaking words which already have meaning. Theoretically it is possible for a child to have a limited capacity for associative learning of the type required in reading. A child, for example, may be a relatively good all-around learner, but have a constitutional limitation for making the associations between printed words and meanings. The tests devised to detect this difficulty require the child to learn to associate certain visual figures with the ideas conveyed in one case by a picture and in the other case by a spoken sound or word. These tests really require the child to learn a number of words in what is essentially an artificial language. In John's case these tests were particularly significant because a previous examiner had said that the boy was probably suffering from injury to certain associative areas in his brain as the result of a severe fall which he had suffered some years before. But John was quite able to learn associatively to "read" the artificial languages. This was satisfactory evidence that he had no brain defects or constitutional deficiencies preventing associative learning of the type required in reading.

The examination thus far has surveyed the possibilities that John's difficulty in reading was based upon organic or constitutional deficiencies of some sort. Since it has shown rather conclusively that these are not at the root of the matter, the examiner is now justified in seeking the cause of the difficulty in the field of acquired defects or inappropriate techniques. An adequate examination, in fact, involves a very careful survey of the many subtle techniques which are required in normal reading.

In the series of tests of techniques are included examinations of several types. The child's speed, accuracy, and comprehension in both silent and oral reading are measured. Due to the fact, as mentioned above, that John was almost incapable of reading connected material, these tests provided an opportunity to observe his special difficulties. It was found, for example, that John required an unusual amount of time to work out the recognition and meaning of many words observed in isolation or out of context. His progress upon the same words incorporated in senseful materials was so slow and labored that he was unable to make sense out of the passage, even if he did succeed in recognizing some or many of the words. The examination is also so arranged as to enable one to discover to what extent the subject makes use of context clues, such common visible elements in words as *ing, er, st,* and the like, and to what extent the subject is able to translate single letters into their equivalent sounds, or such phonograms as *re, th, br, ought,* and the like into familiar sounds. It was found that John could not consistently identify the common visual elements and that his phonetic translation was extremely labored and ineffectual. It was also found that he made numerous misrecognitions of words, and that these mistakes were not of one, but of many types. For example, he would call *that* either *the* or *they* or in some cases *at* or *her*. A word like *was* would sometimes be reversed and called *saw*, but in other cases it would be called *as*. Words like *on* might be called *in* or *no* or *not* or *or* or *and*.

Without describing all the possibilities, it may be said that the examination showed clearly that John had failed to learn the most essential techniques of word perception. He had not acquired the technique of sweeping a word through from the left to the right and of observing the first part of the word first. Sometimes he seemed to see the tail end of the word first and to study it in reverse order, that is, toward the left; in other cases, he seemed to note first the middle of the word from which he might advance to the end or go backward to the beginning or, he might jump from the initial to the final part of a word. He apparently observed words in the indiscriminate manner that you and I probably observe faces. In observing faces most of us do not have any systematic order of attack; at least we do not systematically go from the left side of the face to the right. We are likely to look more or less irregularly over the configuration. This technique may work quite well in the recognition of faces but it works very poorly in the recognition of words. In fact, in John's case this seemed to be the primary difficulty. He had not developed the systematic, left-to-right progression across the face of a

[51]

word, and he had not learned to recognize the many telling features of word-forms which most of us use, such as the general configuration, conspicuous features, and common elements.

Since no other special difficulties could be found in John's case except those arising from his inadequate methods of word perception, the remedial measures recommended consisted in forms of training designed to guide the boy in the reorganization of his methods of word perception. The results of the training may be stated briefly as follows. On October 21, 1923, when the pupil's age was 8.5 years his reading ability was substantially zero. On January 10 in the following year, when he was 8.7 years old, his reading ability had developed so rapidly that his reading age was 8.3 years, or in other words, 95 per cent of his chronological age. On May 1, 1925, when the boy was 10.1 years old, his reading age was 12 years. At this time, his reading ability was 19 per cent above the average of children of his age. On December 9 in the following year, when he was 11.7 years old, his reading age was 15.2, a score 30 per cent above his chronological age, and what is still more significant, 12 per cent above his mental age. Here then is a case in which the psychological examinations enabled the child, who probably otherwise would have been doomed to educational oblivion, to reinstate himself completely. In fact, this child changed from one who was able to make little or no educational progress, despite considerable talent, to one who was able to achieve results which were high even for a person of his already superior native endowment.

Diagnosis of General Educational and Personality Maladjustments

The diagnosis of disabilities and the management of remedial treatment in reading, spelling, arithmetic, writing, and other tool subjects has now become a specialty in itself. Progressive public and private schools have experts on their staffs for such service. Closely related to this work is another type of diagnosis which deals with general school difficulty rather than with a disability in a particular subject. The diagnosis of general difficulties usually falls within the province of an officer called the school psychologist. I shall offer an illustration of the type of problem a school psychologist is called upon to solve and indicate a characteristic type of approach. It is the case of a girl whom we shall call Mary, in the fifth grade of a public school. At the time of the examination she was ten and a half years of age. Her difficulties were reported as follows.

Although she had done fairly good work in the fourth grade, she was now rapidly losing interest in her work and falling behind her class in the fifth. The parents were warned. In fact, they were told that if Mary did not improve immediately and greatly, she would fail to earn a promotion at the end of the year. Mary showed a growing indifference, sullenness and irritability both in the school and at home. Various little changes in her temperament and personality, such as loss of her usual sunny disposition and a tendency to retreat into spells of gloomy introspection, were apparent. It was discovered also that she was slowly losing weight.

The picture here drawn is a familiar one. Such cases of general and progressive loss of interest and ability are frequently presented to the school psychologist whose task it is to find the cause. The difficulty of the task lies in the fact that such a behavior-picture may be the result of many different factors. For example, if the child were of somewhat nervous or unstable constitution, as reported in this case, unsuspected defects in vision might produce all of the above symptoms, including the decrease in physical

[53]

vitality and the change in personality and temperament. Or focal infections, in the tonsils or in the adenoids or in the intestines, might produce similar symptoms. Again, an incipient case of tuberculosis might result in loss of weight and interest and temperamental changes like those here revealed. One of Mary's parents had the idea that a hidden physical disturbance in the brain might be the cause of Mary's difficulty, and indeed it might have been. The endocrinologists have recently shown that many such symptoms as those in Mary's case may be due to abnormalities in the growth or functioning of the endocrine glands, especially the thymus gland. Thus a variety of physical disorders or disturbances might be the cause of Mary's maladjustment.

In such a case as this, one might even suspect that rather mysterious and progressive disorganization of a personality known as a dementia praecox—that is, an early or precocious dementia. In the early stages of this insidious disorder the child may show a growing degree of indifference, more or less negativism or irritability, and other changes in personality and temperament. Although this disorder does not always take this form it sometimes develops as early as the tenth year and shows a clinical picture similar to the one here found.

In cases of this sort the school psychologist makes a careful investigation of the preceding life of the child both at home and in school. His interpretation of the findings is likely to differ from that of an investigator of the Freudian or other schools of psychoanalysis, but he is interested in substantially the same data. In almost any case of this sort it is usually possible to secure reports of unusual experiences in the child's history. Mary's mother reported several very shocking experiences which Mary had encountered. The first, and perhaps most important one, was the unfortunate illness and death of a little boy who had been Mary's almost exclusive play-mate for several years. The mother reported that Mary lived in a world of melancholy and gloom for some time after this experience. This seemed particularly significant to the mother because she had heard that such emotional experiences, so painful to recall, were often labored with and finally repressed into a region known as the unconscious, where like mischievous animals they strove to break forth into the upper conscious region. She had also heard that such experiences after being buried alive for many years might still be the cause of serious forms of mental disorder. Indeed the story in this case might have been grist for the Freudian mills had not another and more plausible explanation of the child's behavior been found.

It is true that the psychologist, like the psychoanalyst, is also interested in the relationships between the child and its parents, and in this case it soon became evident that the mother had necessarily assumed the responsibility for the child's early management. She admitted quite frankly that she had rather "babied" Mary, and that the child had developed an unusually close attachment to her and great dependence upon her. She had always shown unusual concern about her and had perhaps tended to prolong her period of infancy. From experiences of this sort a psychoanalyst might build up a considerable explanatory structure to account for the later difficulties in school. Using a quite different explanatory approach, the school psychologist simply recognized the fact that this child had repeatedly resorted to the care and affection of the mother whenever faced with difficulties during her younger life. Since she had developed habits of thus seeking her mother's protection, it was now likely that if, for one reason or another, she should receive rather severe treatment in school or encounter trying problems of any sort, she should retreat from the real issue by some

[55]

device that would provoke her parents' attention and sympathy. The device might be mere expression of resentment against the school, complaint against the school officers, or the development of emotional symptoms which might in turn so interfere with the bodily processes as to produce loss of weight, energy, and interest. Hence a sort of psychoneurotic retreat from reality might have been the most conspicuous causal factor in this child's difficulty.

Of course, difficulties such as this may also be due to mismanagement on the part of the teacher and the school psychologist must make a careful investigation of the pupil-teacher relation. It is possible for a teacher so thoroughly to misunderstand or to mismanage a child as to make the child's normal progress or adequate adjustments in school almost impossible.

A further cause of difficulty, and one of the most common sources of difficulty in school, is often revealed by the intelligence test. The picture in Mary's case is similar to that shown so frequently by pupils whose intelligence quotients are about 80 or 85, that is to say, 15 or 20 per cent below the average. Such children often get along very well in the first two or three grades, but generally begin to fall behind in the fourth grade and to have real difficulty in the fifth. Finding the work beyond their intellectual comprehension, these children are likely to lose interest. As they are often either ridiculed or bored, they are quite apt to develop a distaste for school. In fact those of somewhat sensitive nature may develop emotional disturbances which in turn may actually affect their health and temperament. In short, many may show exactly the symptoms reported in Mary's case.

All these are illustrations of different causes which may lead to the same sort of difficulty. The task of the school psychologist is to ascertain, whenever possible, what the precise cause is, for the proper remedial treatment in one case may be very different from that required for others. The possibilities in Mary's case are now before you. Make your own guess as to what the true cause is.

Mary was finally examined. Competent physicians studied the physical organism and reported no evidence to lead one to believe that the school difficulty had its origin in defective vision, diseased tonsils, endocrine disorders, or other physical bases. There remained the possibility suspected by her mother, namely, that Mary was of unstable emotional and neural constitution. This had indeed been suggested by the family physician who had observed rather unusual symptoms in the child in infancy. One of the first psychological examinations, therefore, was a survey of the emotional and nervous traits. For this purpose the school psychologist uses a careful inventory, or series of questions and tests, besides making observations and studying the case-history records. A thorough investigation of this type failed to confirm the early suspicions. Indeed the evidence suggested that Mary was not and never had been of unstable constitution. On the contrary, she seemed to be unusually well-balanced emotionally and mentally—excepting, of course, the particular disturbances which has recently appeared.

Next in order was the psychological examination of intelligence. Most students of psychology on the basis of the details I have given thus far would suspect that this was simply another case of low intelligence. It may be remembered that Mary when examined was ten and a half years of age. The examination began with the tests on the eighth-year level, all of which she passed. The psychologist proceeded next to the ninth-year level and found that Mary was also successful on all of the tests for that age. Similarly she passed every test at the tenth-year level without an error. If you suspected stupidity as the cause of Mary's difficulties, you now see that your diagnosis is in danger of being wrong. When the twelfth-year series of tests were tried, Mary went through them without an error. Indeed I may summarize the examination and the diagnosis by saying that the only thing that could be found abnormal about Mary herself, was that she possessed an I.Q. of 150, which is found only in about one child in ten thousand picked at random, and is, as you know, about 50 per cent above the intelligence of the average child.

To indicate the significance of this finding it is necessary to mention now certain facts that were previously omitted. The first of these is the fact that, due to the advice of the physician who had attended the child soon after birth and who had noticed some precocious manifestations which were, I believe, mistaken as symptoms of instability rather than as symptoms of high intellect, the parents had kept the child as much as possible from contacts with other children and from school until she was nearly nine years old. Indeed, at the time of the examination Mary had been in school only a year and a half. During the preceding nine years, her parents, fearing that confinement to mental work would injure her supposed delicate, nervous constitution, had kept her so far as possible from reading books and from engaging in other scholastic activities. During a large proportion of this time, adults were her only companions. Accordingly, we have here the case of a child who had been denied schooling until the age of nine, and yet the test revealed what many persons did not suspect, namely, that she had a most unusual intelligence. The values and limitations of the Binet test and other intelligence tests are much discussed, as well as possible fluctuations in the I.Q. and the influence of educational advantages upon it, but if such tests never do more than they did in this case, their use seems amply justified.

Mary's school difficulties may be better understood when it is realized that her conversation, for the first nine years of her life, had been mainly with adults. She had an extraordinarily sophisticated adult vocabulary, adult sentiments, and adult expressions which were a mystery and an annoyance to her teacher. When questions were asked, she gave what seemed to her to be the best answer. To the teacher, these answers seemed highbrow and "smart aleckish," so that she was disposed to misunderstand or to ridicule Mary's best efforts. For illustration, here are examples of this ten and a half year old girl's answers to certain parts of the Binet test. When asked to define the word envelope, her definition was, "An envelope is a double-sheet container with a flap." When asked to interpret a picture which shows a woman sitting in a chair weeping and a man with his hand on the door, her interpretation was, "This man has asked the lady to marry him. But she has had to refuse him, and now she is indulging in the ladies' pet indoor sport of crying." Apparently one of the lessons that bright pupils must learn in the elementary school, as well as in college, is that they must not give their answers in forms that are over the heads of their teachers.

This case, by implication, throws a flood of light upon many of the stories of men of genius who were apparently dull in school. While it may seem incredible that a child can fail in school because he is too bright for the work, there are nevertheless many cases in which this is true. Such an explanation is probably more applicable to our many stories of early dullness than the notion that bright people may be dull in youth, or that they are usually unstable and freakish. Such studies as those reported in Terman's "Genetic Studies of Genius" are, of course, rapidly clearing up all doubts on this question. While all sorts of difficulties and deficiencies as well as all sorts of talents and abilities may be combined in one personality, the typical genius is likely to be a little superior to the average person in physique, in morals, in emotional control, in breadth of interest, in health, and in other respects.

The Curriculum

Among the investigations in psychology which have had a tremendous influence upon educational theory and practice, must be included the studies of the problem of formal discipline, made by Thorndike and Woodworth in 1902. At that time, educational theory and practice were largely founded on the idea that the mind consisted of a number of powers or faculties which it was the main task of education to improve. The school should devote itself to developing memory, imagination, will, reasoning, and other powers. It was assumed that these faculties had an organic basis which might be compared to a muscle and that systematic and rigid training would develop the power as a whole, as the muscle is developed by any one of many sorts of formal and exacting exercises. This general theory led to the development of the curriculum which included a large number of problems introduced not because of their direct utility or even their reality, but because of the mental exercise which they provided. In many cases it was assumed that the more formal and difficult and exacting the mental work, the more beneficial the results. Guided by such a theory, the curriculum was narrow and formal in character and contained a large number of such problems as the following, which I am taking, with certain modifications, from E. L. Thorndike's "Psychology of Arithmetic."[1] First are certain problems, which to quote Thorndike, "would occur in real life only in an insane asylum."

Alice has $\frac{3}{8}$ of a dollar, Bertha $1\frac{1}{16}$, Mary $\frac{3}{25}$ and Nan $\frac{3}{4}$. How much have they together?

[1] By permission of the author and The Macmillan Company, the publisher.

Consider the following ingenious method of finding how many pints there are in a large pile of nuts. The problem is as follows:

There are 9 nuts in a pint. How many pints in a pile of 6,789,582 nuts?

By implication, the child is advised first to count the nuts in the pile and then the number in the pint, and divide the former by the latter.

Consider the following clever way suggested to the child as a means of finding the thickness of a board:

A nail 5 inches long is driven through a board so that it projects 2.419 inches on one side and 1.706 on the other. How thick is the board?

Offer the following problem to any sensible farmer and ask him how often he has been required to figure it out:

Just after a ton of hay was weighed in market a horse ate 1 pound of it. What was the ratio of what he ate to what was left?

Consider also the thoughtfulness of this horse in eating exactly 16 ounces of hay.

The studies published by Thorndike and Woodworth in 1903 resulted in a complete overthrow of the older educational theory of formal discipline. In place of this doctrine was offered the theory of transfer of training, which, in brief, states that improvement in thinking, reasoning, neatness, honesty, and the like is to be found in the development of innumerable particular habits, and that these habits are likely to remain imbedded in the situation in which they are developed. A corollary to the theory is that such habits transfer from a situation in which they were developed to other situations roughly in proportion to the degree to which the two settings have elements in common. This doctrine at once led to the educational

[61]

theory that the school should attempt to teach primarily those facts and skills, attitudes and habits which are required in the affairs of everyday life.

The impetus given by this revolutionary doctrine led rapidly to a host of studies designed to determine the frequency and importance of operations in arithmetic, facts and principles in history and science, and information and skills required in other subjects, in the lives of children and adults as they are today, or, as they are likely to be presently. In one such study made by a student of Professor Thorndike, Dr. G. M. Wilson, a survey of the actual arithmetical operations used by representative adults in all walks of life and in all the activities of life was made. This investigation showed not only that the arithmetics included an enormous amount of fantastic and misleading problems, like those cited before, but a large number of operations, which, though of value to certain specialists, are rarely if ever used by a typical child or adult. The following are examples: The greatest common divisor and the least common multiple, long and complex problems in compound fractions, reductions to denominate numbers, apothecary weight, computation of the square and cube root, problems in proportion, problems in ratio beyond limits set by fractions, problems in mensuration, such as those concerning the trapezium, polygons, spheres, problems in discounts except as they are concerned with United States money, partial payments, compound interest, and many others.

Similar investigations have been made in other fields. For example, spelling books in common use fifteen years ago often included as many as 7,500 words, a considerable proportion of which were such demons as the following: *marasmus, hychopathy, varioloid, quassia, valerian, badinage, chirography,* and several more difficult ones that many people today would hesitate even to pronounce in public.

[62]

What to teach in spelling has since been determined by counts of millions of words found in the written composition of children of all ages, and of adults. As a result of extensive investigations of these types, it has been found that approximately four thousand words comprise about 98 per cent of those used in the written composition of both children and adults. Such words as the demons listed above are not written once a year by more than perhaps one person in a million. It is, of course, a sheer waste of time to teach all of the children to spell all these words, which they will never use and probably never understand. It is furthermore true that study of such words is a less effective means of developing spelling ability than study of the words that one will actually use in writing.

All along the line the misleading formal and futile materials have been eliminated from the curriculum, with the result that there has been an enormous reduction in the needless difficulties in the elementary school. On the other hand, the curriculum has been tremendously broadened. Instead of struggling despairingly with problems and exercises introduced merely because they were difficult and therefore presumably designed to improve the mind, the children are now engaged in learning facts about food and clothing, hygiene and health, the nature of the physical world immediately about them, how to get along with each other, the significant facts of social, political, and economic institutions, and other things that will be of vital importance in their everyday life.

Methods of Teaching

In the modern school the materials used are so closely tied up with the methods of using them that it is difficult to treat either in isolation. Most readers of this volume have probably had sufficient contacts with some type of progressive school to realize that the methods of teaching

[63]

and working are very different from those in use two decades or more ago. In the development of modern methods of teaching and learning, investigations in psychology have been basic. Since there are many varieties of so-called progressive schools, some of which appear not to be fully in line with principles of psychology, it may be well to illustrate a type of program which seems to me to put into effect satisfactorily the principles of the psychology of teaching and learning.

As an illustration, I shall take a unit of work as I actually observed it recently in the first grade of a near-by public school. In this unit of work several characteristics may be observed. First, learning goes on in the midst of a broad and rich program of artistic, dramatic, constructive, exploratory, and other enterprises. Second, all these activities are organized so as to lead toward some important final result, such as a day of festivity. This, of course, is designed to give the children from the beginning a tangible and desirable objective so that the work throughout the period will be motivated and purposeful. Third, the older types of subjects—reading, writing, spelling, and arithmetic—are not taught as isolated lessons, but are combined and related to each other in the pursuit of some extended enterprise. Fourth, the most careful attention is given to the development of the basal skills in reading, writing, and the other tool subjects. These skills, however, are developed not through the old-fashioned formal drills and narrow types of memory work, but as a natural and necessary result of doing the practical things that the situation calls for. Fifth, the activities are so organized that each secures exercise in school in the way that it will naturally be used in life elsewhere. For example, oral reading is not used as a means of teaching children the mechanics of reading. It is freed from this distortion and exercised only when it serves its natural function as when a child, who has first

[64]

read silently some selection which may be interesting and valuable to another, then reads the selection aloud to a really interested auditor. Finally, the program in all of its elements is appraised in the light of its intrinsic appeal to children's interests. This does not mean that the curriculum is turned over to the whims of momentary interest, but that, other things being equal, it is composed of those materials and activities which make the greatest appeal.

In the particular unit of work which I shall comment on here, all of the activities are organized under one general topic, The Circus. The work begins with the teacher introducing the general topic. This she does by displaying in a prominent place on the board a large colored drawing of a clown. One of the children observes the clown and asks questions about it. The teacher then leads a general discussion of circus affairs. A suggestion is thrown out that the children might make plans in preparation for a circus which they may later give for their friends. Since this is a theme and an enterprise that appeals to the children, they at once set to work. The teacher then listens to the various suggestions offered by the children and writes on the board those of their comments which contain words and ideas that may be used later.

Once the topic is introduced, the children are given a series of exercises contained in a Work Book. These exercises have been carefully prepared beforehand to achieve a number of educative results. In the first place, each page introduces a number of words that the children will need to read in order to explore the available literature concerning the circus. For example, the first page (see Fig. 1) introduces such words as *elephant, monkey, clown, circus, ring.* After the exercises on this page have been completed, the children receive another similar exercise which reviews the words first introduced and presents certain new ones (see Fig. 2). It will be noted also that this exercise contains many facts and suggestions about the circus. Its character suggests the development of a circus poster. The page, in

CHAPTER TWO

Lesson 1

This is an elephant.
Color the elephant.

This is a monkey.
Color the monkey.

This is a tent.
Draw a line around the tent.

This is a clown.
Color the clown.

This is a circus.
Color the circus.

This is a circus ring.
Color the picture.

Copyright, 1930, by Arthur I. Gates and Miriam Blanton Huber

FIG. 1.

fact, contains its own directions, so that the work with it is largely self-manageable, even in the first grade. The children proceed and execute the directions as given. These direc-

[66]

tions call moreover for artistic work such as drawing or coloring pictures. The pictures on the page contain sug-

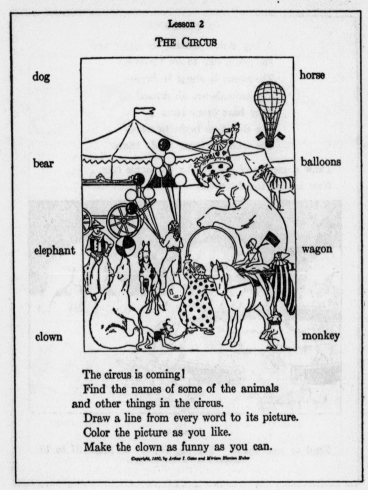

FIG. 2.

gestions concerning circus costumes, circus animals, circus stunts. Further pages carry on this developmental work (see Figs. 3, 4, and 5).

[67]

It should be noted also that each of these pages provides some form of expression of comprehension of the material

Lesson 3

A boy stands outside the circus tent
He would like to see the circus
The circus is about to begin
The animals are all dressed up
They have funny suits
The elephants begin to march
The monkeys begin to do tricks.

Draw a picture of the boy by the circus ring.
Now he can see the circus.

Lesson 4
Read in your reader "The Big Show," on pages 37 to 40

Copyright, 1930, by Arthur I. Gates and Miriam Blanton Huber

FIG. 3.

read. In Lesson 6, for example, reproduced in Fig. 4, the child is required to show his comprehension of the material by drawing a picture. The teacher can tell by a glance at the completed picture how fully and accurately the child has comprehended the selection. If inaccuracies

Lesson 6

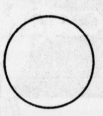

Make a clown's funny face.

This ring can be his head.

Draw his eyes, mouth, and nose.

Make him a funny cap.

He wears a funny collar, too.

Can you put a collar around his neck?

Now color the clown so that he will look fine.

Would some orange color help

to make him look funny?

Let the other children see your picture.

FIG. 4.

appear, the teacher knows that the child needs further work with the words and concepts introduced on this page, or on the preceding pages. The child, in other words, is

[69]

diagnosed without being required to submit to one of the older, rigid types of examination. He is really unaware of

Lesson 7

IN THE CIRCUS RING

This is the circus ring.
The Clown and the Elephant are very funny.
All the people are laughing.
They like to see the big Elephant stand on the barrel.
They like to see the clown, too.
It is fun to see him put the stick and the hat on his nose.

> Color the barrel black.
> Color the hat yellow.
> Color the stick green.

Lesson 8

Read in your reader "Baby Elephant and the Red Cap," on pages 41 to 48.

FIG. 5.

being examined. He has merely proceeded to do the natural thing in the situation. If the child shows adequate comprehension, it is a signal to the teacher that he is ready to go ahead.

The materials in such exercises are also organized in such a manner as to introduce the new words almost automatically and to develop all of the basal mechanical skills required for highly efficient reading. Thus the child acquires adequate perceptive habits, proper eye movements, and phonetic skills without having to resort continually to the older type of narrow, formal, dull drill, such as isolated word study, phonetic exercises, word dissection and the like. Instead the child acquires his technical skills in the process of natural, full-fledged reading itself.

Each series of activities of this type prepares the child to read a story which is contained in a Story Book or Reader. At certain points, the child is given directions to turn to his Reader and read a particular story or selection. Due to the fact that the preceding exercises have introduced every new word and all of the technical skills required for free and intelligent silent reading the pupil is now able to read the story silently without interruption or without being taught or harassed in the process. Thus the teacher is not required to do what, until recently, she has had to do, namely, to tell the story or require the children laboriously to read it in a group exercise before they read it silently.

After a number of the children have completed their silent reading of the story, they are given a page of comprehension exercises (see Fig. 6). After these exercises have been completed by some of the children, they are taken up in a group discussion and different responses noted. This exercise provides a diagnosis of the fullness and accuracy of their understanding and appreciation of the story. In some cases, children disagree concerning the contents of the story. This disagreement provides a natural incentive for rereading and rediscussing the story—a very different procedure from the old-time order to "read the story again." For children who show weaknesses, additional work is given by the teacher

---

Lesson 11

Draw a line under the right answers.

1. What can you see at a circus?
   Clowns and elephants.
   Cups and electricity.
   Carrots and eggs.

2. Who lived in the circus?
   A Baby Elephant.
   A baby beaver.
   A blue dog.

3. What did the Baby Elephant want?
   A circus ring.
   A red cap.
   A red collar.

4. What did the clown give Baby Elephant?
   A blue coat.
   A black collar.
   A brown cat.

5. What did Jingo fall into?
   A barrel of coal.
   A barrel of cold.
   A barrel of tar.

FIG. 6.

A few such exercises give the children a substantial introduction to the general topic which will, as a matter of fact, be pursued for three weeks or more. From the materials read and discussed, the children secure suggestions for all sorts of correlated activities. In these enterprises, they may be permitted to exercise their own ingenuity and thus develop initiative and originality. They will secure experiences in making and executing plans directed toward a remote goal. Many of them are, strictly speaking, self-initiated enterprises which provide freedom for creative and constructive work for which the modern schools make such a plea. The work, however, is not altogether individualistic, but on the contrary, cooperative, for the reason that although children may specialize according to their interest and talents, they are all interested in the same topic and aiming toward the same general objective, the development of a class circus.

In the school in which the work was observed, some of the children were engaged in making large posters on which they drew and colored pictures and wrote phrases and sentences. Others began at once to construct costumes for the clowns, for the elephants and other animals which they were interested in introducing into the circus. Others began to work on stage materials and apparatus, such as decorated tubs for the elephants to stand on. Others began to write small posters and invitations. Some wrote verse about circus affairs; others wrote stories; still others were interested in developing a dialogue for a dramatic event. Some of them made preparations to rehearse a circus stunt. The teacher in charge of physical education, instead of requiring the pupils to do the ordinary gymnasium work, arranged to give them equally healthful and much more interesting and educative exercise in the form of rehearsing their stunt for the circus.

Meanwhile, the teacher in charge of the library, at the children's request, had selected all the books suitable for first-grade reading that were related to the circus topic.

[73]

These books were made easily available to the children who came in in groups. Due to their intense interest in the circus enterprise, these pupils eagerly viewed all the pictures and read all the stories that could be found. In such work, oral reading found its natural purpose when one child having discovered an interesting selection read it aloud to the others. Some of the children, at the suggestion of the teacher, began to prepare the copy for the circus edition of the First Grade News, which was published as a mimeographed sheet on the day of the circus.

Meanwhile the children have been exploring their entire environment for everything related to their circus and circus events. They have explored the attics of their homes for costume material, and the nearest museum or zoological garden to learn about the animals. For example, some of them wanted to find out precisely how the ostrich walked, lived, and in general had his being. Observing the ostrich, one of the children trained carefully to imitate his curious step and learned much about the ostriches in freedom and captivity. By incorporating all of these educative activities in one fairly prolonged enterprise, interest in the topic was not nipped in the bud, but allowed to develop and flower.

Near the time when the topic had reached a full exploration, the unit of work was brought to a close in a day of festivities in which everyone in the class participated, and to which their friends were invited as guests. On this day the children's activities were not limited entirely to dramatic activities, as important as they are. The gymnasium, in which the circus was given, was decorated with the products of the children's work. Among these were many materials which contained reading and other problems. Being interested in each other's work, the children were eager to read or otherwise to appraise the various things that had been achieved. When the first-grade newspaper was distributed, the children read it with full interest, despite many competing appeals. Due to the fact that they had all read so widely on the same topic, they were nearly all able to read these new materials accurately and fluently.

A modern program of this type is really not only more interesting and more educative in a broader sense, but really more efficient in securing the same technical skills that were previously sought by the formal, rigid drill programs. It is important to stress this point, for the reason that it is quite common to find criticisms of the modern school in this respect. Let me offer as an illustration the achievements obtained in reading in a first-grade class taught by a program similar to the one just described.

In one such instance, two large first-grade classes comprising forty-one and thirty-eight pupils respectively were taught by typical public-school teachers in a small town in Pennsylvania. They gave no more time to reading as such than is given in the typical traditional public school. In one of the classes, in which the average intelligence was exactly 100, the children showed an attainment in all the basal skills in reading at the end of the first school year which was equal to that obtained in the traditional school only after twice as long a period of instruction. There was not a failure in reading in the class. Some time before the end of the year was reached, the children were able to read and interested in reading full books by themselves. The average number of books read by the individual pupils in this class was in fact twenty-two. In the other class, which contained less mature pupils of lower intellectual levels, the I.Q. being only 88, similarly superior results were obtained. The average child in this group read fourteen full books. Thus it appears that the newer methods do enable children to acquire greater reading ability than ever before by a method far more enjoyable.

It should be pointed out in passing that the function of the teacher in such a program is very different from what it was under older methods. The teacher is no longer a slave driver. She is, in fact, scarcely a teacher in the older sense of endlessly forcing children to learn against their will. As John Dewey has expressed the theory:

It is no longer a question of how the teacher is to instruct and how the pupil is to study. The problem is to find what conditions must be fulfilled in order that study and learning will naturally and necessarily take place, what conditions must be present so that pupils will make the responses which cannot help having learning as their consequences. The pupil's mind is no longer to be on study or learning. It is given to doing the things that the situation calls for, while learning is the result.[2]

There are, of course, many so-called progressive schools which do not follow a program of this type. In many schools organized primarily for experimental purposes in which results have been carefully measured as far as possible, certain deficiencies have been revealed. For example, a method used in several progressive schools, frequently called the opportunistic method, differs from the one which I have illustrated with approval, chiefly in the lack of careful organization for the purpose of insuring the development of the basal educational skills. Only a few years ago such an opportunistic program was set up in a famous school for the purpose of experimental comparison with a more systematic organization similar to the one I have outlined. The achievements of a first-grade class in many phases of education—reading, writing, spelling, arithmetic, general information, self-initiated activities, social, emotional, and other habits and attitudes—were measured and appraised as objectively as possible. To give only one illustration for purposes of comparison, it was

[2] From an address, "Progressive Education and the Science of Education." By permission of the *Journal of the Progressive Education Association*, Washington, D. C.

found here that the opportunistic procedure, while it enabled many children to learn to read with marked skill, also resulted in almost total failures in almost 20 per cent of the group: whereas a procedure similar to the one just described resulted in no failures and in an appreciably higher average attainment. While some of the radical procedures found in occasional progressive schools probably suffer from lack of system and organization in the curriculum, from depending too much upon children's immediate interest and initiative, from permitting pupils to spend too much time in relatively uneducative, playful busy-ness, the more intelligently directed modern school has demonstrated the fact that a program of absorbing interest can be organized so as to achieve greater development even of basal skills than can be secured by the older types of formal laborious drill.

When one considers the fact that scientific studies arising from psychological research have made it possible even now to relieve the curriculum of formal content amounting to a third of the total required fifteen years ago, and the further fact that many more eliminations are possible and that the newer methods, such as those I have described in reading, have already doubled the returns per unit of time in comparison with methods used fifteen years ago one may reasonably expect that in the not distant future the fundamental school subjects will be developed better than ever before in one quarter of the time formerly required, and that thus a large portion of the school day as well as the teacher's energy will be conserved for broader educational work.

Adult Education

So far we have been concerned with problems arising in the school system as it now exists. Educational psychology has uncovered facts which indicate the importance of

[77]

education before and after the conventional school period and which suggest important reforms and alterations in educational programs and agencies throughout its whole length and breadth. Since the significance of education during the preschool period has been covered by other contributors to this volume, I shall leave the cradle and approach the grave. Indeed, I wish I had more space in this chapter to devote to adult education, its possibilities and relations to the conventional system of schooling, for I believe there are vast possibilities in this field for effecting most important advances in human welfare.

Psychology has always been interested, indeed at times chiefly interested, in the mental processes and organic adjustments of adults and considerable work has been done on the capacity of adults to learn and to adjust themselves to social, vocational, civic, and recreational environments. Studies made within recent years, especially those by Thorndike, have revealed the unrealized practical importance of adult education in meeting the demands of modern life. Thorndike's work has shown convincingly, for example, the error of our older idea that the years from six to eighteen represent the period of maximum learning ability and that the period from thirty to fifty represents a time when one is too old to learn. The decade of maximum learning capacities in all those tasks which require intellectual facility and retentiveness is from twenty to thirty; the period from thirty to forty is superior to the ten- to twenty-decade, and the span from forty to fifty is only slightly inferior to that from thirty to forty. Popular opinion and recently enacted policies in many businesses and industries seem to assume a highly erroneous view of the capacity of old dogs to learn new tricks. Even in sheer memorizing, in acquiring simple associations requiring little or no judgment or in developing motor skills which conflict with habits previously formed as in learning a new language, the adult in the forties is a match for his offspring in the teens and is exceeded only slightly by those in the prime years, the third decade of life. In general, persons beyond the age of forty are still able to learn. In fact, they can probably learn some things more rapidly and more thoroughly than they could when they were in the elementary school.

There are reasons, moreover, for believing that the adults' deficiencies in learning may largely be overcome. They may be due in part to lack of confidence and lack of practice. They are fostered by our educational tradition—the idea that only youth can learn— and by the educational system —the scheme of consolidating education entirely in the years from six to eighteen or more, and then quitting it completely. The recent investigations suggest that this long-established system succeeds admirably in confining education almost entirely to the school period and in discouraging the individual and social agencies from attempting adult education. The same investigations imply, however, that a far better system would provide facilities and incentives for education from twenty-five to fifty at the very least.

There is evidence that many school subjects, such as history, science, philosophy, economics, literature, and others may, in considerable measure, be learned more effectively after thirty-five than before. There are doubtless many vocational activities, now denied to adults over forty, which may be learned as well and as rapidly after thirty-five as before. There are probably some industrial and business enterprises in which the adult above forty can excel persons of younger years. The more carefully psychologists and educators study the relations of competence to age, the more certain they become that the growing tendency to refuse employment indiscriminately to older men is an unwise and preventable economic tragedy. There are reasons for believing that if an industry explores the possibilities of adults of forty or more by scientific methods, adjusts its machinery and devices to their nature and puts into effect efficient methods of training them for new tasks, it may harvest a rich reward. Industry has in considerable measure made many older people incompetent by the simple device of adjusting the work to the younger ones, especially through the "speeding-up" process.

In general, the recent investigations suggest the desirability not of dividing life into two sharply divided periods, a period of school and a period of work, but of providing educational agencies for the whole period of life. They suggest also the fallacy in the notion that a man can learn only one vocation and that only when he is young. If the future brings as radical changes in industrial life as the past fifty years have brought, we should have agencies for vocational selection, guidance, and reeducation in recognition of the entire feasibility of learning a new vocation at intervals of ten years, more or less, as conditions demand. Thus, what is perhaps the most hideous and disturbing phobia in America today, the fearful uncertainty concerning one's livelihood after forty, could be replaced by a confidence that would do more to make life happy and fruitful than anything that can be achieved by all our present political and industrial makeshifts combined.

Chapter IV

THE FOUNDATIONS OF PERSONALITY

by MARK A. MAY

THE study of personality is by no means the special province of psychology. Other interested and active sciences are anthropology, biology, chemistry, genetics, neurology, psychiatry, sociology, and to some degree paleontology. Contributions to the scientific literature of the field have come in from all these sources especially during the past fifteen years. The total contributions in number of books, articles, reports, and dissertations will run up into the thousands.

I shall not attempt to summarize nor appraise this body of literature. To do so in the brief space afforded here would be a foolhardy undertaking. I shall, however, attempt to locate the major problems, indicate certain methods of approach, and try to gauge the progress that has been made in their solution. Before beginning this task it will perhaps clear the way to consider briefly the meaning of the term personality.

The word personality comes from two Latin words, *per* meaning through and *sonare*, to speak: hence *personare*, to speak through. The noun *persona* was first used, I believe, to indicate a mask worn by actors to which was attached a kind of megaphone through which they spoke their parts. Later the word was used to designate the part played by the actor, and hence the characters in the play were called *personae dramatis*.

[81]

According to this it would appear that personality means the part that each of us plays in the drama of life. This is true enough provided the dramatic aspect is not so overemphasized as to introduce a notion of ostentation or of pretense which was probably not present in the root meaning of the word. The *persona* or megaphonious mask was not thought of as something that hid the player but rather as something which gave him distinction, which made his voice heard distinctly—in short, it was that which made him effective.

Thus, according to the original meaning of the term, personality is that which makes one effective, or gives one influence over others. In the language of psychology it is one's *social stimulus value*. Every individual may be regarded as a stimulus to every other individual with whom he comes in contact. The kind of a stimulus he is may be measured by the way others respond to him. If he is a "weak sister" in the sense that his presence or absence makes no difference in the behavior of others, then he has a weak personality; if on the other hand his presence or absence makes a big difference in the conduct, ideas, and attitudes of others, then he has a strong personality.

Modern psychology seems to have departed rather widely from this view of personality and from the root meaning of the term. J. B. Watson defines it as "an individual's total assets (actual and potential) and liabilities (actual and potential) on the reaction side." F. H. Allport defines it as "the individual's characteristic reactions to social stimuli and the quality of his adaptation to the social features of his environment." These two definitions are typical of those found in current textbooks on psychology. While the various definitions differ in many respects, they nearly all agree in placing the emphasis, as Watson and Allport do, on the reaction side. The notion seems to be that an individual's personality may be completely de-

[82]

scribed in terms of *his reactions*. This view of personality is a direct outgrowth of behavioristic psychology in its endeavor to get away from psychological entities and subjective categories.

The view presented here is a re-emphasis of the root meaning of the word and holds that personality cannot be completely described in terms of reactions but that the individual as a stimulus must also be taken into account. An individual's personality is not defined wholly by his responses to others but also by the responses that others make to him as a stimulus. It is true that the individual's stimulus value is composed of an integrated series of variables including such things as physique, dress, manners, quality of voice, choice of language, and many other types of response including his characteristic social reactions. To the sum, or parts, or combinations of parts of these variables others respond. It is these responses made by others to the individual as a stimulus that define his personality.

This view is quite in accord with the common-sense view taken by the man in the street. The adjectives popularly used to describe personality are such as attractive, forceful, strong, magnetic, or their opposites. These adjectives are not descriptive of the individual's social reactions, but rather of him as a social stimulus. When asked to describe an individual's personality one does not begin by giving an inventory of his reactions, but rather by describing the impression he makes on others, or by describing the way he influences others. Indeed, many personality-rating scales employ adjectives that are mainly if not wholly descriptive of the individual's stimulus value.

Personality traits are usually viewed as response values, but they also have stimulus value. For example, if an individual assumes an air of superiority and impresses others as refusing to associate with them, he is said to be snobbish. But his snobbishness is not something that he possesses but

[83]

rather something that is inferred from the way he carries his cane, or wears his necktie, or speaks to others. Others react in a more or less unified and similar manner to certain of his responses or to his appearance or presence, and these responses of others are taken (or rather mistaken) for traits possessed by him. His traits are not possessed by him but are in fact his constant stimulus values.

The view of personality here presented does not deny the reaction side but insists that the stimulus side be included in the picture. Personality is thus a two-sided concept. On the reaction side it is the integration of the individual's characteristic and persistent reaction tendencies, habit patterns, modes of conduct, or ways of adjustment; on the stimulus side it is his social effectiveness, or influence on others. While these two phases of personality are inseparably tied together, they are not wholly identical. It is true that one's stimulus value is determined to a great degree by one's reaction patterns, yet other factors such as physique play an important part. On the other hand, it is also true that these characteristics and persistent reaction patterns are determined in part by one's stimulus value, and in part by other factors.

Is it possible now to deduce from all this a short and snappy definition of personality? Definitions are tricky and dangerous especially when attempted for broad and nonscientific terms. One of the rules of definition is that an object cannot be defined in terms of itself. But when the object is so broad that it covers everything like itself, what is there to do? It is like the famous question on the college philosophy examination in which the students were asked to define the universe and give two examples. Personality is a concrete reality, like the universe of physics from which the scientist abstracts certain qualities for study. As a working hypothesis, personality might be characterized as that total organization of reaction tendencies, habit patterns, and physical qualities which determine the individual's social effectiveness.

This preliminary excursion into the field of definition seems justified on the ground that it may dispel some of the fog hovering over this type of inquiry. Let us now review some of the scientific problems of personality that have been attacked, and indicate briefly the methods of approach.

The aim of all science is the *adequate description* of the subject matter with which it deals. The criterion of adequacy may be anything you like but it is usually prediction and control. Thus we arrive at the rather trite observation that the ultimate aim of all personality studies is the prediction and control of individual and group behavior. The immediate aims of the vast number of studies mentioned above are, of course, many and varied. Fully 90 per cent of them take the reaction point of view and are thus concerned with the description of some aspect of behavior or with some trait of behavior, attitude, or opinion. The remaining 10 per cent may be said to be concerned with the social stimulus side of personality. My view is that the proper object of study is not the individual whose personality is being investigated but rather the responses of others to him as a stimulus, but since study of one personality by measuring the responses of others to it is relatively rare in the literature, we shall turn at once to the more numerous direct studies of human behavior.

One of the favorite indoor sports (and most sciences are just that) of the personality investigator is to select some behavior pattern, or trait, or attitude, or attribute of the individual, define it roughly and then proceed to study the extent to which individuals differ in it, the conditions under which it is present or absent, and the ways in which it is related to other features of the individual's external or internal environment. The particular trait or attribute may be a relatively narrow one such as speed of decision, or caution in doing an examination, or neatness of dress. On the other hand, more ambitious workers fired with a zeal to tackle more pressing social problems will choose more inclusive and more complicated traits such as delinquency or economic success. A brief list of the so-called personality traits that have thus far been investigated includes aggressiveness, ascendance-submission, caution, complacence, confidence, conformity, conscientiousness, decision-speed, expansion-reclusion, deception, honesty, inhibition, originality, preservation, persistence, self-assertion, self-assurance, self-control, service to others, social perception, suggestibility, and trustworthiness. This is a brief list of conduct traits and does not include a much longer list of attitudes, interests, preferences, prejudices, desires, emotions, instincts, moods, ideals, ideas, and motives; nor does it include abnormal types of behavior which are of interest to the psychiatrist, nor the mob or crowd types of behavior which are of primary interest to the sociologist. It merely illustrates the fact that the data of most personality studies are in terms of human responses. The aim is to describe these responses as accurately as possible and in scientific terms, with an ultimate view to prediction and control.

But high levels of reasonable predictions as to whether X will be more honest than Y, or how long Z will remain faithful to his wife, or whether a political candidate is a strong enough social stimulus to get himself elected, are yet in the distant future. Science proceeds slowly and by stages.

In the field of personality study there are at least three stages of progress. At each stage there are important problems. The first stage is that of qualitative descriptions of the subject matter. The observer notes what happens and records it in any convenient terms. The problem is that of recording what an individual actually does in various situations of life as he meets them in his daily routine. To the ordinary layman this looks to be a very simple and easy task. But let him try for example to make any kind of a record of the precise movements of any individual for the period of one hour and he will soon come to the conclusion that it is a very difficult job. Nothing is more elusive and difficult to pin down than the ordinary activities of every-day people in everyday life. If there is any further doubt about this, go to any criminal court and listen to a trial in which precise movements of persons become an important part of the evidence and see how hard it is to establish the facts.

The second stage is that of noting trends, likenesses, differences, clusters, or nuclei in the observed behavior. This is the hypothesis-forming stage. Suppose the observer notes that John Doe exhibits a typical pattern of behavior in a certain type of situation. It may be that at parties or other social gatherings he talks loudly, laughs heartily at his own jokes, and in other ways endeavors to make himself the social center of gravity. The hypothesis is formed that he possesses that personality trait known as egotism. Or suppose again it is noted that the average height and weight of senators, bishops, college presidents, and auctioneers is considerably above that of the average run of the population. An hypothesis is immediately formed that height and weight are important factors in determining one's social stimulus value. Or, if it is noted that men of small stature tend to speak loudly and roughly to their inferiors, or tend to be bombastic in other ways, then the hypothesis may be formed that these behavior patterns are compensatory mechanisms and lead to peculiar types of personality. In each of these cases a trend is noted and conceptualized.

The third and final stage in the scientific study of personality is that of measurement. If there is such a thing as an

[87]

inferiority complex it should be possible to measure it; if extraversion and introversion are true personality traits they ought to be measurable; and the same may be said for such qualities as selfishness, caution, courage, honesty, and the like. Furthermore, if there are individual differences of a quantitative sort between different personalities in respect to their *social effectiveness*, such differences should be susceptible to measurement. But when one talks about measuring such a complex affair as character or personality the hard-headed man of common sense immediately grows suspicious. Lord Kelvin was probably right when he said that measurement is the highest stage in science.

These three stages of science with their attending problems may be summarized in the form of three questions: (1) Can the behavior of individuals in daily life be systematically recorded? (2) Why do they act as they do, or how did they get that way? (3) Can human behavior be measured to the degree that will permit of reasonable prediction and control?

Although description, hypothesis, measurement, and prediction represent the sequence of science, this sequence is an ex post facto affair. As a rule scientific inquiry does not complete one stage before passing on to the next. Qualitative description, conceptualization, and measurement usually go along together. Yet on the other hand this sequence will serve very well as a pattern for determining the work that has been done, and also in estimating the present scientific status of personality studies. What then do we know about personality scientifically? What progress has been made? How far along the road of scientific progress have we really traveled?

At the level of qualitative descriptions of behavior patterns on the one hand, and total personalities as social stimuli on the other, there are vast quantities of literary data but few that are truly scientific. Biography, drama, fiction, and anecdotal history are full of such descriptions. But there is little here that is grist for the mill of the scientists. The scientist wants either a large number of observations of the response of a great many persons to the same situation, or else a large number of responses of the same person to the same or slightly variant situations. In this literature such records are lacking.

The scientific cupboard is not, however, entirely bare. The anthropologists, for example, have made rather detailed records of the gross observable features of the conduct of primitive people; the psychiatrists have accumulated vast quantities of data concerning behavior manifestations of persons whose conduct deviates markedly from the accepted social norms; sociologists have collected no end of case histories; economists have described types of behavior involved in the satisfaction of the major human wants; psychologists have collected millions of test scores and laboratory records of narrow ranges of behavior. Yet in spite of all this it is an amazing fact that basic data for the study of personality and character, that are usable by science, are very meager indeed. As an illustration of the scarcity of truly scientific data bearing on practical problems of human conduct, consider the number of textbooks that have been written on ethics, the number of sermons that have been preached on honesty, and the number of codes of honor framed by schoolboys and Rotary clubs. Yet no one, until a very few years ago, had made any serious and systematic effort to gather such simple facts as the kinds of situations in which people are deceptive, and how deception varies from one situation to another. The same could be said of all the virtues and vices which underly American business and American life.

Further evidence of the lack of the scientific data that are basic to a fundamental understanding and prediction of human behavior is seen in our inability to cope with

[89]

the outstanding problems of human failure. We are now in the midst of a great economic depression and no one knows the causes thereof. It is true that it was predicted in a way, but its fundamental etiology is unknown; or again, the annual toll of human life taken in industrial and automobile accidents increases, yet the causes of accidents lie hidden in the dark corners of human nature. It is true that we have conquered diphtheria, yellow fever, diabetes, and pernicious anaemia; but we have not yet slain the dragons of bankruptcy, graft, war, unemployment, poverty, and bootlegging.

We may well ask why it is that we know so little in a scientific way about the plain facts of human behavior. One of the reasons is that we lack scientific tools for gathering data. We have many more scientific facts about the behavior of wasps, bees, frogs, chickens, rats, rabbits, and apes than we have about human behavior, for the reason that animals cannot talk to us. Being unable to communicate with them by language we have been forced to develop techniques for close observation of their behavior. When we want to know something about the behavior of a spider we watch its behavior and devise an elaborate system of note-taking for recording our observations systematically. But when we want to know about the behavior of our fellow man we either ask him or ask someone else, or give him a test, or get him to answer a questionnaire.

But this is not all. Language is a further handicap to the progress of science in another way. Philologists tell us that the English language was not invented by a committee of scientific men appointed by some primitive royal society. Natural and biological scientists became aware of this fact long ago and invented a language of their own, drawing heavily on the Latin and Greek. But the psychologists and social scientists still stick to Noah Webster's dictionary. The result is that it is well-nigh impossible to describe human behavior in terms that are precise and unambiguous. Most of the adjectives in the English language that apply to behavior are explanatory rather than descriptive. We are left with the alternative of describing behavior in very formal circumlocutions, or describing it functionally in terms which by their very nature tend to explain it. An example of this difficulty is given by Dr. D. S. Thomas in one of her attempts to objectify observations of the behavior of children. The observers found it easy to count and record the physical contacts between children, and two or more observers agreed in their counts; but when it came to classifying these contacts into pushes, pulls, slaps, or embraces there was much diversity among the records of the different observers.

There are in general two major types of descriptions of behavior, the formal and the functional. Within each there may be recognized subtypes. Formal descriptions range from those in terms of physics and chemistry to those in terms of stimulus and response; functional descriptions range from stimulus and response terms to those couched solely in terms of purposes, desires, or other explanatory concepts. Thus the functional and formal are general types found at the opposite extremes of a scale. The mechanistic biologists and the extreme behavioristic psychologists hold that all behavior can be adequately described in the language of physics and chemistry and that when the detailed story of all the physical and chemical changes has been told nothing more can be added. The objectivistic psychologists and biologists hold that the story cannot be adequately told in terms of physics and chemistry alone but that the stimulus-response formula, or some modification of it, is necessary. The purposive psychologists and the vitalistic biologists hold that something even more than the stimulus-response formula is necessary and that some

[91]

language descriptive of the seeking, striving, self-regulating aspects of behavior must be added.

The real issue is whether or not the complete story of any act of behavior can be told in purely formalistic terms. Of this there is considerable doubt, and there is even more doubt as to whether adequate description of the social effectiveness of an individual can be given in a formal way. It may be that we shall never wholly escape the necessity of using explanatory language in the description of behavior. The procedure may require that formal language be used in the first instance and when concepts are formed, that they in turn be used as descriptive. Thus by a continual cut-and-fit process we may arrive at satisfactory descriptive categories.

But my purpose here is not to solve these problems. It is merely to locate them. The problem of finding a straightforward objective way of systematically recording and describing what humans or animals actually do in varied situations is a real one, and must in some measure be solved before the study of personality can become scientific.

The conclusion which the discussion up to this point implies is that there is as yet no substantial foundation of fact on which a scientific understanding of character and personality may be based. We started out by saying that personality is here conceived as an individual's social stimulus value. The underlying facts, which it is the first task of science to get, are facts of human behavior, reaction systems, habit patterns, attitudes, prejudices, desires, and the like, in other words, to find out what human beings actually do in the situations of daily life. This task has scarcely begun.

The second task of science is to find out why human beings behave as they do, why certain individuals have a greater social stimulus value than others, why some function better in their social contacts than others. There are three main avenues of approach to this problem and each approach leads to a different answer.

First, there are those who say that we behave as we do, or that we got the way we are, by virtue of certain behavior mechanisms that have been developed within us. All of our conduct, ideas, attitudes, abilities, and hence our characters and personalities may be explained in terms of inner forces or mechanisms. These forces or mechanisms have been variously named as complexes, repressions, instincts, urges, drives, will power, beliefs, interests, desires, sentiments, predispositions, sets, determining tendencies, motives, tissue wants, contractions, and other devices of the imaginations of the investigators. The idea is that all our behavior patterns, reaction systems, modes of conduct, and types of adjustment are somehow causally connected with one or another of these internal mechanisms.

Therefore the answer to the question of why we behave as we do, and why personalities vary in strength or effectiveness, is to be found in an examination of how these mechanisms are acquired, if indeed they are acquired, and how they operate. What is wanted is the "inside dope." The kind of dope that comes out depends to no small degree on who it is that goes after it and the techniques that he uses in teasing it out. A few years ago science witnessed an epidemic of glands. When the physiologists and biochemists discovered or thought they had discovered some of the functions of the endocrines the pseudo-scientists immediately jumped at the conclusion that all behavior and all personality could be explained in terms of the functions of the antonomic nervous system which controls the secretions of the endocrines. There was much talk of the chemistry of character. It was thought that character was achieved by gaining voluntary control over the smooth muscles of the body by the simple techniques of conditioned reflexes. If we could only somehow control our "insides" and could teach children this trick, many of our social problems would be solved. But now that we know more about the functions of the endocrines, and more about the complexities and frailties of conditioned reflexes, we are not so certain that the foundations of personality have been discovered.

But the real expert on inner mechanism is the psychoanalyst who is sure to go to the bottom and bring up an explanation not only of human behavior but of human institutions as well. He has manufactured for himself a large stock of explanatory terms which he calls behavior mechanisms that dwell within us and force us to perform all sorts of odd tricks. The names of these supposed inner mechanisms are such familiar household expressions as complex, repression, sublimation, projection, ambivalence, identification, fixation, compensation, resistance, and libido, to mention only a few. There is truly no form of human behavior and no event in history that the agile psychoanalyst cannot explain by the simple process of selecting from his list a few explanatory terms that fit the case. The fallacy of explaining a complicated process by giving it a name, and thereby setting at ease the mind of the inquirer, is very common in psychoanalysis. Even orthodox psychologists have been guilty of it.

The chief difficulty with the psychoanalyst is the way his mind works. His greatest scientific sin is that of the preconceptualization of his data. He observes what seems to be a common element running through several situations and appearing to be basic to the conduct found therein. He immediately conceptualizes this observed trend or nucleus and calls it a name, and then goes on to assume that he has found one of the foundation stones of personality. Thereafter he uses this concept as an explanation not only of the type of behavior in which he observed it but also of other types to which it might conceivably apply.

I come now to the psychologists. Being a member of that labor union I am more inclined to give it a clean bill. Most of us are believers in the importance of inner mechanisms, even the most hardened behaviorists. We vary however in the kinds of inner mechanisms that we hold as basic to personality. There is the ancient clan of instinct-mongers who believe that all human behavior and achievement, all character and personality, has its ultimate basis in instincts. But instincts as an explanatory hypothesis have recently grown odious and unpopular. They have been vigorously and even viciously attacked. Whether they will weather the storm yet remains to be seen. In this connection it is a curious fact that the very psychologists who threw McDougall's seven instincts out by the front door, immediately took in by the back door seven times seven equally mysterious visitors in the form of urges, drives, impulses, and determining tendencies. One is reminded of the parable in the New Testament in which a man cast from his house a devil who went out wandering in the wilderness and solitary places and straightway took unto himself seven other devils more evil than himself and returned to the house. The story ends by saying that "The last stage of that man was worse than the first." But whatever may be the condition of the house of the believer in instincts, it now seems fairly certain that the foundations of personality are not to be found among any metaphysical entities.

There is another group of psychologists who pin their faith on reflexes and the mechanisms of the cerebro-spinal nervous system. But even here they split into camps. Some are attracted by the phenomena of integration of the nervous system and feel that somehow this ought to be used as an explanatory device; others look upon the processes of inhibition as the cornerstones of personality. There are probably as many theories concerning the basis of human behavior as there are psychologists who have tried to formulate one. Surely they are not all wholly true and sound. But in the absence of sufficient data it is difficult to pick the right one. For the present at least the safest course is to admit that the psychological foundations of personality are not completely known.

A second type of approach to the explanation of how personality and character are achieved is from the point of view of the external environment. This is known as the situational approach and is sponsored mainly by sociologists and by some psychologists. The notion is that most of human conduct as well as ideas, ideals, and attitudes are due in no small part to the external environment; and what any individual does at any one moment is the direct result of the circumstances that determine the situation. This point of view does not deny the presence, reality, or importance of inner mechanisms, but holds that they are products of environment, and especially of social environment. Thus the object of study for the understanding of personality is the family, the gang, the neighborhood, the business office, factory conditions, living conditions, and other similar environmental manifestations. As an illustration of the importance of the influence of environment on personality it would be claimed that a boy who is brought up by two maiden aunts and compelled to dress up daily and play with little girls, would surely develop a personality different from that which he would have developed if he were one of four brothers, with both parents living, reared in comparative poverty, and ran with a gang.

The social-environment theory of the development of personality is at present a very popular one. It pictures the new-born infant looking up into the face of its mother or nurse and responding in its crude way to her smiles and fondlings. Fully nine-tenths of the child's early social stimuli are mother stimuli, for the mother supplies most of his wants. His basic habits of sleep, eating, digestion, as

[96]

well as his early traits of dominance, aggressiveness, gregariousness, selfishness, and the like are all products of the way he is handled. Thus the foundations of personality and character according to this theory are the habit patterns formed in the early months of life through the everyday processes of feeding, sleep, and handling. Someone has called this the "home products" theory of personality.

It is at the higher age levels that the situational approach is most valuable as an explanation of behavior. One particular brand of it is known as the doctrine of specificity. This doctrine is based on the observation that human behavior varies as the situations vary. Change the situation ever so slightly and you change the response. The basic fact is that conduct seems to be more closely correlated with variations in the situation than it does with inner mechanisms. Stated in a very extreme fashion the contrast between this theory and the inner mechanism theory is that the situational theory holds that when the situation is varied the response is varied even though the inner mechanisms remain constant; whereas the inner mechanism theory holds that when the inner urges or motives or instincts, or what not are varied the conduct is varied even though the external circumstances remain the same. But here again the questions at issue are not settled because the necessary facts are unavailable.

A third approach to an understanding of human behavior and other factors in social effectiveness emphasizes the cultural backgrounds of the individual. It admits that most behavior is the immediate result of the social environment acting on the individual and setting in motion the inner mechanism, but it goes back of all this and points out that both the inner mechanisms and the social environment have a history and can only be accounted for in the light of this history. In brief it is the phylogenetic approach.

[97]

This approach has two main avenues, both leading backwards to a more primitive and elementary state of affairs in search of the foundations of personality. One avenue leads back into biology, the other into cultural anthropology. The strictly biological approach to personality seeks the antecedents of the inner mechanism; the strictly cultural approach seeks the antecedents of social environment. There is a group of physiologists, comparative neurologists, psychobiologists, and others who believe that the foundations of human behavior and therefore of human personality are to be found in the fundamental mechanisms of lower animals. Therefore, in order to understand the behavior of man we must first understand the behavior of animals. It is a curious paradox, but nevertheless true, that we have learned more about the mechanisms of human behavior by studying insects, rats, cats, dogs, and apes than we have by studying men, women, and children. There are several reasons why this is true. One which I have already mentioned is that animals cannot talk to us. Another is that we can experiment on them in ways that we cannot on human beings. And still another is that the behavior of the lower animals is presumably less complex than that of man.

The cultural approach, which is concerned with the historic backgrounds of social environment, is more social and hence more interested in the stimulus side of personality. Its data are more in the nature of group activities. There is no doubt but that a large portion of human behavior, ideas, beliefs, opinions, and preferences are determined by customs, codes, and social standards. Language, music, art, fashions, religion, etiquette, and other similar affairs go to make up the culture of a tribe or nation. These cultural factors not only condition personality, but they are in a real sense part and parcel of it. In a recent study of the organization of character it was found that a child has almost as many characters as there are social groups of which he is a member. Furthermore the group appeared more important as an integrating factor than any inner mechanisms that could be discovered.

Cultural patterns influence personality not only directly but also indirectly through a very efficient process of education. The child inherits all the mores of the group in which he is born in the sense that he is powerless to change them. Social education is mainly a process of conditioning the individual to the cultural patterns of his group or nation. Different individuals react differently to these patterns and social standards and thereby achieve differences in personality. From this point of view the foundations of character and personality are mainly cultural. The problem of human behavior is not only one of mutual adjustments between the organism and its social environment, but also between the inner mechanisms of the organism and social traditions.

To sum the matter up, what are our conclusions concerning the foundations of personality? The answer is that the entire foundation has not as yet been uncovered. The situation is somewhat like that of digging up the ruins of an ancient city. One group of archeologists begins at the south wall, another at the north, and still another at the east and west. One group finds the foundation to be of stone, another finds brick, and another finds brick and stone and perhaps concrete, and each comes to a different conclusion concerning the material and structure of the whole. But when the whole thing is uncovered they find that each was right but no one was wholly right. So it is with the foundations of personality. A group of psychologists, psychiatrists, neurologists, and physiologists who by training and temperament have become interested in inner mechanisms and their biological antecedents believe that the foundation stones are in the shape of reflexes, habit patterns, muscle tensions, tissue wants, metabolisms, or else in the shape of instincts, impulses, urges, drives, complexes, motives, and the like. Another group of psychologists, psychiatrists, sociologists, and cultural anthropologists who by their training and temperament have become interested in the social environment and its cultural antecedents find the foundations of personality in group codes, social standards, family adjustments, living conditions, economic standards, or else in culture patterns such as customs, mores, types of language, beliefs, superstitions, and other manifestations of social traditions.

No one has yet to my knowledge attempted to bring together in one volume all the scientifically established facts concerning personality and character. I have already indicated that the literature is voluminous but the facts are few. New truth is being dug up daily and each year more and more of the foundations are exposed. The most fruitful years lie ahead.

Although the prediction of the outcome of any great scientific adventure is very hazardous, I am willing to guess that when enough facts are in to reveal the outlines of the foundations of character and personality they will appear somewhat as follows. The biological sciences with their emphasis on the mechanisms of behavior will enable us to understand those broad and universal types of conduct such as eating, sleeping, mating, reproduction, care of children, fighting, and the like; but they will not enable us to understand why the Scotch are both canny and stingy, if indeed they are, or why the Hindus are meditative and reflective, if they are, or why the Swedes are stolid or the Latins temperamental. Such racial differences in personality, if they really exist, will be better understood in terms of social environment and culture patterns. But neither inner mechanisms nor social environment will enable us to understand such individual differences in character and personality as we are able to observe within any one group. Every individual is a different sort of social stimulus, and every individual has his own peculiar behavior patterns, attitudes, ideas, and opinions. To describe adequately and fully account for these individual differences all the resources of both the biological and social sciences will be required.

Chapter V

PSYCHOLOGY AND THE PROFESSIONS, MEDICINE, LAW, AND THEOLOGY

by WALTER R. MILES

Spirit and Aim of the Professions

IF, when driving your car in traffic, your foot chances to slip from the brake to the gas pedal this little extra motion may occasion the strenuous activity of the major professions in your behalf. A doctor may have to hurry to keep you out of the morgue; a lawyer puzzle to keep you out of prison; and a minister counsel and pray to rescue you from the slough of despond. Health, respectability, and faith, these three, and there is no use trying to settle the matter which is the greatest. Law, medicine, and theology represent so many kinds of attempted aid extended to individuals and to groups to the end that maladjustment may be rectified and normal adjustment more certainly achieved in the various life processes and relations. No one wishes to live in a country that is not amply manned by competent physicians, lawyers, and ministers. But at the same time, no one quite likes to fall into their hands. Keeping the doctor away, neglecting the lawyer, and listening to the preacher at the safe distance of a radio transmission set are generally typical of our ways. The reasons for this natural shyness between the potential patient, client, or parishioner and the practicing expert are not far to seek, but partly they are short-sighted and founded on a false psychology. The spirit and service of these professions in their work with and for society is best typified by that from which they have sprung in the beginning, that is, the parent-child relationship. If a child asks its mother for bread will she give it a stone? The trouble is the child and the patient usually ask for cake.

For one thing it is the relative isolation of the great professions, one over against the other, that makes them fearsome. Each profession naturally seeks territory for itself, develops its own principles, formulas and procedures, and arranges these, barricade fashion, presenting a bold and rather aggressive front to society. Then, too, a profession creates for itself a kind of psychological enemy which it professes to fight, and no one quite likes to think of himself as the highway on which this traffic and stamping of combat will take place. In the nature of the case professional activity must usually be counted upon as a means of earning a livelihood. There is here a very real psychological illusion, a misjudgment tendency on the part of nearly all who are serviced. The professional expert holds himself in readiness for call. The client does not want to pay for the "holding" or "the readiness," but only for the call and quite moderately for that. The person suffering from this high-pay illusion will say to you in true psychological nonchalance, "It isn't that I mind paying him ten dollars for ten minutes' time, but while I was with him he did not give me his uninterrupted attention, he answered the telephone, spoke to the nurse, and jotted down memoranda about somebody else." And so it is that some say the professions are so many kinds of robbers, preying upon people whose acute and chronic distresses put them in a dependent position. Thinking men and women must combat criticisms intended to besmirch and destroy our most constructive agencies. One thing is certain, adults must adjust their ideas of recompense for these maternal-like services to a grown-up business basis, and quit thinking in terms of "mother nursing and waiting on me for nothing."

Medicine deals in a most intimate way with a matter that has always perplexed religion, philosophy, and psychology, that is, the mind-body relationship. It seeks to keep both of these in health and in harmonious adjustment. Law concerns itself with the citizen-state relationship, and in America is essentially individualistic in spirit. Its object is to protect the rights of the individual and to let them develop freely. Theology concerns itself with the individual-universe relationship. This involves social relations with fellow men and adjustment to the ideas and concepts of ultimate ends. These professional domains and concerns are not artificial or arbitrary. They spring directly from the mental characteristics and behavior of man. They are a boldly sketched portrait of our own psychology without our recognizing it. Humans, the world over, show this feature of group psychology and naturally hit upon these three professions as regularly in the same way as they make for themselves the cutting knife, the weighing balance, and the written word.

Wherever and whenever men have written out the code of behavior for members of these professions, the statement has represented the highest ideals of the human mind, a kind of Sermon on the Mount, a program to challenge the whole energies of a man. Recently there was published an English translation of a Japanese medical code.[1] It is the Koan Ogata Scroll. The Japanese physician, Ogata, lived from 1812 to 1863. This is a part of what he had inscribed on his scroll.

1. The physician lives not for himself but for others. This is the essence of his profession. Do not look for fame or profit. Work to save others though you lose yourself. Maintain life,

[1] Koan Ogata's Fushi Ikai No Ryaku, translated by Shiro Tashiro and Martin H. Fischer, *Journal of the American Medical Association*, Vol. 90, pp. 1151–1152, 1928.

restore the sick, and ease the suffering of men. You have no other object.

2. Face to face with a patient, remember only that he is sick, not his station or his wealth. Compare the rich man's handful of gold with the poor man's tear of gratitude. Which will you have?

3. When practicing your art remember that the patient is the target, not the bow or arrow. Do not play with him. Think without prejudice; consider with narrowed eyes.

4. Besides being modern and erudite, learn how to win the confidence of your sick man through word and action. But let these not be superficial, casual or pretentious. Do not mouth deceptive and queer hypotheses.

5. At night think over the happenings of the day. Record your experiences and observations. Such benefits the patient and the world.

. . . .

7. Even when the disease is incurable, understand the sufferings of your sick man and do your duty by trying to maintain his life. It is inhuman to surrender. Even when you cannot save him, you can comfort him. This is a human art. Try to prolong his life, even though it be but for a moment.

8. Make the patient's illness cost him as little as possible. Of what use to save his life when you take away the means of his maintenance?

. . . .

10. Respect the older physician and endear the younger to you. Stress their better side and refuse to comment on their treatment since you have not seen the patient.

Statements like these declare the motivating ideals characteristic of all these great professions that endeavor to serve us.[2]

The Psychology of Professional Specialization

If it is just to say that philosophy is the mother of the sciences it is perhaps equally true that religion is the mother

[2] WILBUR, RAY LYMAN, The Honor System in Medical Practice, *Journal of the American Medical Association*, Vol. 89, p. 570, 1927.

of the professions. The patriarch of the tribe or the priest of the group, as preserver and purveyer of the sacred objects, customs and rites of his followers, in primitive society and early civilization, naturally combined within himself the duties of pastor, lawyer and doctor. He was the shepherd and leader of his people. The psychological laws of ascendancy-submission are ever operative in social groups and the leaders attempt to do about the same things in all ages —because now as in the earliest periods of history they are working with humans. When the medicine of the early Greeks first took form it was in the hands of the priests of Aesculapius, the god of healing, and there were temples of healing located at different places. The priest used drugs and did some surgery and used other medical procedures but these were strongly flavored with religious factors.[3] According to mythology, Aesculapius, whose daughter was Hygeia, after whom all the hygienists take their name, was considered the greatest physician of all times, and I guess we should say he must have been the most able and most efficient practical psychologist who ever lived. For the story is this, that Pluto complained to Zeus that the happiness and prolongation of life on the earth brought about by the ministrations of Aesculapius were seriously reducing the population of Hades. And Zeus, in order to get things back to their traditional status, had to kill Aesculapius with a thunderbolt. This accomplished the wishes of Pluto, the King of Hades, but it gave medicine and particularly psychology a terrible setback.

The medical man was the first professional split-off from the priesthood. Religious features tended to be abbreviated and even to fall away in that behavior that had the more

[3] Two classes of people were discriminated against: those who were moribund and women at the time of childbirth. These were not allowed in the temple enclosure. We may suppose this was partly for psychological and mental therapy reasons; both groups would be particularly disturbing to the others who came for treatment.

specific and remedial aim. I think it was a psychological wedge that brought this split, and the individual sufferer constituted the thin edge of this wedge. When the priest and sufferer were in each other's company there grew up a mutual concern that was something different from the temple routine and had in it the seed of experimentation and science. And so through various stages it came about that priest and physician more or less parted company. But the latter did not forget immediately all his priestly ways. The laws of habit and the psychology of invention do not permit such clean jumps. For example, he might continue to use the impressive healing proverbs. When applying a bandage to a wound he might say, "Of wounds, for wounds, a blessing"; or, "Stop thou thy bleeding"; or, "Thy stinging, thy swelling, thy torturing, thy raging, thy stinking, thy festering, thy running shall cease!"[4] Psychologically this was of course enough to help any ordinary difficulty and to some extent even the extraordinary ones. Today the psychological counterpart of the healing proverbs is in the doctor's or nurse's cheerful expression, "I think that will fix you up all right."

After the split-off of the physician from the priesthood the next psychological stage is reached when the doctor belittles the abilities and ways of the priesthood to emphasize the distinctness of his profession, a kind of psychological civil war which there is no need to discuss at length. Law of course has usually had to wait for church and state to divide in order to afford the proper chance for the development of an independent legal profession, separate and distinct from the general advising and directing social agencies.

The fundamental characteristics of the human mind and its preponderate tendencies in remembered experience show themselves in the successive appearance of the sciences and

[4] GARRISON, F. H. "History of Medicine," 4th ed., p. 50, Philadelphia, W. B. Saunders Company, 1929.

the professions. The objective ones come first and so are given leading emphasis. This seems modeled on the plan that we give greatest attention to what can provide visual experience. Astronomy, whose objects of inquiry remain observable from generation to generation, is the first and foremost science. Then follow physics, chemistry, geology, geography, biology, the institutional, the linguistic, the historical sciences, and late or last in the series, psychology as a science. After looking at everything else and hunting for more things to look at and touch, man finally turns to consider how he looks, touches, and thinks and how and why he is acting thus and so.

Divisions and more divisions have come in all the major professions, particularly those that deal with the more materially objective things, as witness the many varieties of engineering based on the classification of materials. Medicine has divided and subdivided. It has divided into specialties along the lines of the natural divisions of the human form, the sensory capacities, the stages of human development, the sexes, the chief functional systems of the organism, the catalogue of diseases, geographic areas, and has found even other differentia for defining the objectivity and giving names to the medical specialties. The surgeon, the anaesthetist, the trained nurse, the pharmacist, and the manufacturer of medical instruments are other types of allied objective specialists. Operation of the same psychological principle has brought about the law specialties but here the divisions have been subgroups, along lines indicated by the kinds of institutions, the different social groups to be served, and the classes of social relations that, because they are what they are, most frequently show instances of maladjustment and need legal advice and direction. The clergy has its bishops, pastors, missionaries, teachers, and professors as well as religious editors and other division chiefs, but in general has not developed professional specialties to the extent that has been typical for law and medicine. Psychological objectivity has not been so generally and convincingly possible here. Although theology has abounded in writings, teachings, and formulations with reference to the nature of man, the nature of the deity, design, love, sin, redemption, salvation, and future state of being, there has not been as large a body of objective, concrete material demonstrable to all mankind as there was available for medicine and law. This is one reason why organized religion tends to go toward edifices and paraphernalia. The Church has claimed to possess the keys of heaven and hell; eye-minded man has wanted them on exhibition. This position of theology, in place of giving rise to new and well-defined specialties within the profession of the clergy has in the past brought forth divisions of opinion with the resulting multiplication of denominations—another psychological variety of specialization. In reference to the more observable relations of man with man there is among all religious groups a fair amount of agreement. The point of view in all civilized countries is characterized by high moral tone and ethical value, calculated to direct the individual's interest somewhat outside his own selfish domain and to promote social progress. Less unanimity of view has pertained in regard to the relation of man to the universe, and in consequence it is chiefly from this side that denominations have arisen. The uniting of some of the larger Christian denominations in the present decade is a movement of great human import.

Whether religious ministry can split off from itself any more major professions is an interesting question. It is quite possible that in the future psychology may be regarded as such, side by side with law and medicine, third and last child of theology and reared in large part away from home. These three should constitute an effective trio for the future, but they never will dispense with the mother from which they have sprung, whose activities will always be general, deeply sympathetic toward man, urging him forward and broadening his horizon.

In brief, professional specialization proceeds not as a freakish phenomenon of social life but according to fundamental psychological laws. The steps might be enumerated as follows:

1. Human beings tend to arrange themselves in groups or swarms.

2. Wherever a group exists leadership and submission develop.

3. Leadership concerns itself with the protection and direction of the lives of those who are led. It must do this if it is to continue to enjoy leadership.

4. The human body, the social body, and the world of mankind are three entities which the mind can see or think. Leadership must help with the difficult phases of all three.

5. The most tangible and specific entity is the human body. If the leadership or servicing is to be divided the natural thing is to set off the doctor first.

6. Professional divisions are set off and also subdivided according to the objective tangibility of the things to be done.

7. The professions struggle among themselves for domain and prestige but serve man best in cooperation.

8. Finally, the more specifically psychological features of life are becoming clarified and tangible. This indicates the setting off of a new profession, that of psychologist, which we believe has within it certain integrative features which will make it a useful colleague for the other professions.

Systematic versus Individual Treatment

The reformers in the professions, in a real sense the psychologists of the past, have always been struggling to convince the professions that man himself should not be forgotten or ground to dust under the systematic routines and machine which the professions create, theoretically, for his service. The words, "The Sabbath was made for man and not man for the Sabbath," were called forth by a widespread recurrent difficulty which is always near at hand. The impetus for the beginning of a profession comes from man's gregarious tendency and the human responses of sympathy and ingenuity in the presence of crying human needs. But once the project is under way, the ingenuity and intellect side may run away with it. Facts, observations, and proposed explanations tend to crystallize into systems. The solvent evaporates and the substance hardens. It becomes difficult to apply it to the irregular features of a human being, and as finally evolved we have a tough, bulky, unyielding mass against which the human beats and bruises himself. The elaboration and building up of systems, attending to them, thinking in their terms and bowing before them, to the partial neglect of individuals, is only another instance of the strong objectifying tendency in the human mind. The prescription, law, or creed that can be put on paper achieves the halo of authority. The body of doctrine that can be stated with a show of logic and with the seeming definiteness of numbered headings, that occupies space and can be exhibited, that can be taught, committed to memory, and commented upon, and in all of these ways made tangible, becomes weighty doctrine. Classification schemes, medical formulas for treatment, court procedure, rites and ritualistic practices, have appreciable good within themselves. Their validity inheres in their usefulness as means of adjusting men, women, and children to life, to one another, and to the universe, and rests ultimately on empirical rather than on theoretical grounds. The famous dictum of Osler, "No man should treat a disease until he has had it," if expanded to

[111]

read, "No man should treat a disease until he has had it or after he has forgotten what it felt like to have it." states the literal ideal we have in mind for medicine. To be able to say, "I had it, I remember exactly how I felt, and I cured it in this way—," is to state about the most joyful news a doctor can bring to a sick patient. But we cannot expect all physicians, lawyers, and ministers to be Jobs and to bear in their own bodies all of the human ills, trials, and sufferings. Always it will be necessary to apply treatments a little blindly. But we want the minimum of such blindness! How to avoid the slavish application of a system, and at the same time achieve and apply knowledge with wisdom—this is the problem. And in this problem we are all more than just a little interested.

Psychological laws of attention and interest prescribe that the specialist shall see phenomena consistently in the meaning and interpretation of his specialty; he defines, refines, and confines himself thus. In general the specialist himself does not contribute greatly to expanding his specialty; others from the outside are more apt to induce new developments. It is a matter of attention patterning and the persistence of mental configuration. You get one scheme in mind for the arrangement of the house you want to build and the architect perhaps offends you because he has other ideas. So it is for the boundaries of science and for the lines of professions; they tend to be scratched in deeply by the men who live within them. It remains for the more playful, adventurous spirits to go exploring across and between borders, irrespective of whose territory they search over. From such as these, mostly, come new insights and the readjustments of system to sympathetic treatment.

There is hardly a better concrete illustration of this for medicine than Ambroise Paré, the great French surgeon who lived in the sixteenth century and was chief surgeon to

King Henry II.[5] He was not educated for the profession of medicine but was a man of very great insight into human behavior, ills and suffering. He perfected himself in the surgical practice of the day in the charity hospital of Paris, and in 1536 became a surgeon in the French army and had his first contact with war injuries. He repented that he had gone from Paris to see so pitiful a spectacle. Paré's attitude, human understanding, and sympathetic treatment are illustrated in the following passage. He had read a book entitled "Of Wounds in General," by Jean di Vigo, and that author had stated that wounds made by firearms were poisoned wounds because of the powder, and for their cure he had commanded to cauterize them with oil, scalding hot. Paré says:

In order not to err before using the said oil, knowing that such a thing would bring great pain to the patient, I wished to know first how the other surgeons did for the first dressing, which was to apply the said oil as hot as possible into the wound of whom I took courage to do as they did. At last my oil lacked and I was constrained to apply in its place a digestive made of yolk of eggs, oil of roses, and turpentine. That night I could not sleep at my ease, fearing by lack of cauterization that I should find the wounded on whom I had failed to put the said oil dead or in poison, which made me rise early to visit them, where beyond my hopes, I found those upon whom I had put the digestive medicament feeling little pain and their wounds without inflammation or swelling, having rested fairly well throughout the night; the others to whom I had applied the said boiling oil, I found feverish, with great pain and swelling about their wounds. Then I resolved with myself nevermore to burn thus cruelly poor men wounded with gunshot.

This principle of adapting the treatment to the patient, of evolving it on empirical rather than on wholly theo-

[5] HAGGARD, H. W. "Devils, Drugs and Doctors," p. 38, New York, Harper & Brothers, 1929. See also DOROTHEA W. SINGER, "Selections from the Works of Ambroise Paré," New York, William Wood & Co., 1924.

retical grounds and of discarding the system even if it were that of Hippocrates or Galen, if it did not work, made Ambroise Paré the ideal surgeon and physician. Paré did not write in Latin; he had not come up through the schools of the profession; hence the medical men of Paris scorned him, organized and propagandized against him. Nevertheless he is one through whom the physicians and surgeons of today would prefer to trace their lineal professional descent. The systematized and intrenched profession if it does not have within itself a forward-looking sensitive minority, responsive to the criticism from the outside, is psychologically doomed. Of what use is it to build great symmetrical pyramids that serve simply to cover up the dry bones of dead men?

Psychology and Medicine

From the very beginnings of the professions there have been physicians, lawyers, and ministers who were outstanding because in addition to the mastery of the knowledge and techniques of their professions they have understood and given much weight to psychological factors, although these were usually not so named. In the reading of medical history and in the practice of medicine today one can see in many places the application or the neglect of these principles. The masters of the past handed on to their successors the more objective and at the same time measurable features of their experiences. They could not so satisfactorily write down or otherwise successfully convey the art side of their professions, which included also their psychological insights. Psychology as an experimental science began some fifty years ago and has gradually accumulated a rather wide range of problems, a variety of techniques, and some quantitatively stated observations, in a rather mixed-up vocabulary. These more or less satisfactory objectifications of human nature and behavior have brought within the bounds of common knowledge what was once included only in the vaguely defined insights of the masters. Considering the age of medicine and the youth of psychology, a presentation of the contributions of psychology to medicine seems about as presumptuous as an errand boy's discussion of his contributions to the financial policy of the banking institution which he serves. But the boy might be permitted to say what he thinks could be done and what he hopes to do when he grows up.

At present a good deal is being written on the subject of the taking of medical histories. Why this emphasis? Consider for a moment the situation of the ordinary practicing physician a generation ago. He is called upon in person by a father whose twelve-year-old daughter is reported simply as "having no appetite." He visits the home. There he finds the grandmother, the mother, the father, the patient, and two other children. While making his rather leisurely visit, an aunt, sister of the ailing child's mother, and one of her children drop in, "just to see what the doctor thinks of Mary." Here, spread out before the eyes of the physician, is a living chart of the nature-nurture background of this individual—like grandmother, like mother, like daughter. Here are racial stock, type, vitality, education, occupation, standard of living, present crisis, all before him, to be comprehended through that most comprehending of sensory channels, the eye, and this almost without asking a question. Then, too, this same physician was present at the birth of this very child, his patient in the present instance, and he has on many other occasions visited the family. There is for him no great necessity of writing down a card full of data and depositing it in a filing system because the whole neighborhood is this physician's filing system, and his display cards and history charts are life-size. Today this condition of affairs has disappeared. Now the more common situation is that

[115]

the physician is called to see the child who has already been isolated in its room. The mother or some other member of the family may be present. Time is precious. The physician can hardly get satisfactory answers to even half the questions he would like to know about. There is nothing else for it, he must accept the case, make blood counts or analyze the sputum in his laboratory, and see whether he can work out a diagnosis from brief but thorough analysis.

The substitution of laboratory analysis for bedside diagnosis and the displacement of one physician who accepts the responsibility of seeing the patient through, by a group of specialists, who in total group of course know much more, tends to hide the individual as such and to make him into a case to be known by number. The modern method probably in most instances works much better than did the older way in getting at infectious diseases and conditions of structural pathology. On the side of functional disturbances, however, particularly those where a strong mental factor is present, the patient seriously needs, after the medical laboratory examination and more urgently than its usually negative results, the psychological aids of personal acquaintance with the physician, confidence in him and respect for him, and assurance of his personally continued help and interest. The psychological specialist is the proper person to assist in this present difficulty. He can help the physician to a more complete knowledge of his patient as relates to habits, temperament, and individual difference.

History taking involves not only overt symptoms but also the more or less unrecognized beginnings of a tendency to distress, psychological and physiological adjustments, changes in routine, etc. The human organism is not a self-diagnosing system. Physicians have always recognized this, and although they ask the patient, "What is the matter with you?" they of course do not expect him to be able specifically to name the difficulty. The organism has no fixed or stationary state of being. It has no standard intensity index. It is a relative system of complex elements. Psychoanalysis is one attempted modern solution for dealing with this situation as relates to mental difficulties and twists that need to be followed back and readjusted. There is no parallel heart analysis or stomach analysis that can be brought into play to reinstate the original disturbing experience and remodel it. Nobody, so far as I am aware, has ever been able to recognize in himself what it was he ate or didn't eat that gave him pellagra. The same is true of all the deficiency diseases, the diseases of allergy, such as hay fever, the serum disease type of disturbance, and of course the digestive, respiratory, kidney, and circulatory disturbances. These conditions and symptoms involve the memory and the trustworthiness of recalled incidents and dates. They involve individually peculiar behavior habits and early training and the testimony of others. All of these things are clearly the characteristic interests and usual subjects of investigation for the psychologist.

Preventive medicine, and especially that part of it which does not deal particularly with public health and hygiene, is a field in which in the future the psychologist will work with the physician. The oft-quoted dictum in reference to the long life of him who has a chronic disease is a testimony in favor of this argument. If the difficulty, weakness, or tendency is discovered early, the human organism may adjust habits and routine suitably, and the modifiability of behavior is such that the individual can live happily, efficiently, and to a reasonable span of years.

In seeking to identify symptoms and to work them out as to sequence, frequency, and intensrty, the physician is at the mercy of circumstances and will secure a somewhat different picture according to different types of temperament, personality, and individual idiosyncrasy. Some will accentuate and stress, others will subordinate and try to ignore items that may be of importance to the physician. When it comes to treatment, the physician in many cases obviously needs to know the intelligence level of his patient and the individual's ability to cooperate in the measures of the treatment, particularly where they involve disturbances of normal routine habits. In such matters as orthopedic surgery, where extensive procedures are to be planned, or in diabetes in children, or in chronic disturbances of the digestive or circulatory system, this matter of intelligence and ability to cooperate on the part of the patient constitutes psychological information of potentially great value. As the older individual can cooperate better than the child, so the more intelligent individual, whatever his age, can help the physician better than the one lower in the scale.

Psychologists have relieved physicians of those cases whose major difficulty lies in mental deficiency, the feeble-minded. These are usually not primarily in need of medical treatment for their defect, although of course they are subject to disease like other mortals. What they chiefly need is to be educated according to their abilities in special institutions under specially trained teachers and by a program arranged according to psychological principles for this particular purpose. This has helped to clear up an old and aggravated problem of medicine.

The field of infectious diseases, from anthrax and the common cold through the list to yaws and yellow fever, would appear to be a not very promising group of opportunities for the application of psychology to medicine. Someone says, "You can't kill real bugs by just thinking about it." But on the other hand there is no point in giving them comfort and aid. Even with infections it is clear that

[118]

the overt behavior of the doctor, the nurse, and members of the patient's family, the psychological fortitude of the patient, and the readiness for psychological adjustment to necessary routine treatment, with confidence and spirited reliance upon the measures adopted, make a difference in prognosis and shorten somewhat the course of the disease and the convalescence. An Indian told the mental side of snake bite in the following picturesque words: "An Indian walks along thinking much about fishing; to his surprise a rattlesnake bites him. He knocks it away, sits down, smokes his pipe, and dozes in the sun. White man walks along, thinking about making money. Rattlesnake bites him. He is much afraid, jumps, shouts for help, runs, worries, and dies. Indian's way is better." I am not sure that the psychology of the patient casts much of a spell over Bacillus Pestis, as the ancient plague of three thousand years' history is the plague, no matter whom or when it hits. But in most instances, as of course every doctor and nurse knows, the patient's state of mind, his emotional life, his motivation, his attitude—all these can be tremendous allies in the struggle for adjustment and renewed equilibrium. As Axel Munthé has said, "There is no drug as powerful as hope."

Although the physician has his ideas of the suitable average dosage for such drugs and therapeutic agencies as he may use, he must always be alive to individual differences and properly alert to interpret especially the language responses of the individual patient. The physician applies a local anaesthetic and says, "How is that?" The patient, relatively somewhat relieved but still actually in pain, may respond, "Oh, I like it!" The physician must immediately interpret and check the meaning of this response through added questions. It is highly important for him to know whether the patient is simply making a conventional social response or whether his words indicate

[119]

a depression of ordinary inhibitors and a more generalized effect than had been intended on the whole nervous system.

In the case of stupors and semiconscious conditions, doctors may discuss with nurses or relatives the patient's condition when in his presence. The assumption is no doubt that the patient cannot understand these conversations. But to the psychologist all such discussions in front of a patient seem absolutely unwarranted. The ear is a wide-open channel to the cortex, open during sleep and approachable from any angle. The human voice, especially when speaking the name of the person is the most challenging stimulus for attention. There must be many instances when individuals unable to exhibit the ordinary signs of motor control indicative of consciousness but actually retaining some auditory sensibility are greatly discouraged by what is said of them in their hearing. The effect is depressing even when it involves no actual bad news, when it simply emphasizes to the patient that he is thought of as outside the social picture, to be talked about rather than talked to or consulted.[6]

There is not space or need here to discuss the more obvious topics of psychotherapy and psychological medicine as represented in the study of the psychotic and the neurotic. The collaboration between medicine, psychiatry, and psychology in the study of these classes of individuals is already an assured program at The Medical Center of New York City, at the Institute of Human Relations at Yale University, and in certain other places. But psychology need by no means be limited to the psychotic and neurotic. There are enormous opportunities in most of the therapeutic fields and we may confidently look forward to the day when each medical service group will have its psychologist as a full-time regular team member.

[6] The same state of affairs exists more or less in reference to individuals who are regarded as insane or intoxicated.

This psychologist will be fully trained and experienced in the techniques of personality evaluation, acquainted with the agencies for adjustment, and thoroughly alive to the need for essential cooperation with the representatives of the other professions in working out the salvation of the whole individual. Where this procedure is already followed we no longer attempt to separate physical, mental, and spiritual, assigning each section of the person to a specialist. Instead the influence of physical, mental, and spiritual stimuli, whether inside or outside the patient, are analyzed in terms of his total organism, his undivided personality.

A short statement of the relation between medicine and psychology which we have just traced is as follows: Psychological principles and practice have always been a part of the successful activity of medical practitioners, but until recently they were unsystematic and therefore not conveyable as scientific doctrine from one generation to the next. In the last few decades two lines of organization of psychological material have led to the building up of a science of psychology in connection with medicine. The first, from within medicine itself, is exemplified in the development of method in the so-called case history. This is an expressed recognition of the necessity of viewing the patient rather than the disease, the total personality with its foreground and background instead of a single sampling or cross section of his physical behavior. Whereas formerly the wisest physicians were bound to come to the conclusion that human beings, not diseases, were their care, now this doctrine is a part of the learned theory of medicine and a systematic study of the patient from this point of view is an important part of medical practice. The second line of organization of psychological material in the interest of medicine has come directly from psychology in psychological laboratories. It has led to a recognition that psychological specialists can contribute to the total picture, and so to the diagnosis, valuable elements that are omitted or only included by chance within the general case survey. Most important for medical practice is the splitting off from it of the care of the feeble-minded, now known to be a purely psychological and educational matter. Equally important for individual human beings is the contribution of laboratory psychology with reference to individual psychological differences and the appropriate types of therapy which they demand. Furthermore, both laymen and physicians can learn from psychology important points with respect to the handling of patients. In most of our largest cities, and in a number of university centers, the need for close cooperation between medicine and psychology has been recognized in the establishment of clinics where patients, not diseases, are studied and treated. Personality development and growth in the widest sense is the purpose of these studies and therapies.

Psychology and Law

Laws have tended to be rather more inflexible than have been the rules of medical practice. The reason of course is no puzzle. In the law two parties must be served—society and the individual—and the compromises or omissions or exceptions are likely to strike one more unfavorably than the other, since the whole situation tends to be a matter of contention or dispute. Individuality is centrifugal. Society is centripetal. These two, we shall not say blind forces, pull and haul back and forth over a theoretically just balance point. In the nature of the case considerable stress may be developed and it takes a long time for the jostling and swinging to subside. Supposedly there is a perfectly just solution and a proper interpretation, and the law, unbiased and inflexibly considered, is to provide this solution. The psychological set-up for

[122]

the carrying on of the law is naturally quite different from that involved in medicine. In medicine, nobody is against you, that is, against the patient, and trying to down him. Every doctor and nurse with whom he comes in contact is more or less solicitous to aid him and to shorten the period of suffering and distress. On the contrary in law, someone must take the role of the prosecutor.[7] This person is then psychologically the enemy of the defendant and is seeking by various means to discover and display the fact that the defendant's actions, attitudes, or relations have been contrary to common standards of respectability and to society's edicts. The result is a combat rather than general cooperation. Veracity is questioned, private relations are flaunted, emotions are aroused, and lifelong enmity created. The mechanism seems a clumsy one and ill-suited to delicate humanitarian purposes and work. In a way it resembles the old schoolmaster, thrashing a ten-year-old boy with his cane to stimulate his interest in drawing and coloring geographical maps. But we must hold that leading jurists have as high ideals as anybody and that it is human psychology and society that make the problem and the process what we find them.

The courts may be slow and law appear inflexible, but it is by no means stationary. Marked progress in the science of codification has taken place in the last thirty years. Switzerland produced a new civil code in 1907, and a revised edition of its Code of Obligations more recently. The Soviet government gave Russia a legislation based on communistic principles, including a Code on the Family, which was published first in 1918 and revised in 1922. In Siam parts of a new Civil and Commercial Code have

[7] This contrast in the professional-social attitudes of medicine and law has been strikingly presented by my colleague Professor Lewis M. Terman, in Psychology and Law, *Los Angeles Bar Association, Bulletin*, vol. 6, pp. 142-153, 1931.

been appearing in recent years. Turkey is said to have a complete modern code dating from 1926. In Italy a draft for a revision was made in 1925, and a commission of French and Italian jurists compiled in 1927 a draft for an up-to-date revision of the Code Napoléon. And, most recently of all, a Civil Code of the Republic of China has appeared, with an English translation of Books I, II, and III, having come from the press in 1930.[8] While occidental legislation has always been essentially individualistic, intended to protect the rights of the individual and to let him have scope for free development, the traditional Chinese laws have subordinated the activities of individuals to the interests of the family. The new Chinese legislation goes beyond this and is a more deliberate attempt to introduce broader social characteristics. The philosophy of behavior underlying the new Chinese code considers men not as self-sufficient entities but in relation to society. The individual must seek his own gratification in such development of his own natural ability as is most likely to contribute to the general welfare. Rights and morals are recognized as purely social notions which may eventually be subject to change and evolution as society itself evolves. The humanitarian temper of this new code is perhaps indicated by the following: "A juristic act, whereby a person profiting by the difficulties, indiscretions, or inexperience of another, obtains an advantage exceeding the consideration for it to such an extent that the unfairness of the transaction is obvious," may be canceled by the court and the obligation reduced. And again, "A right cannot be exercised for the main purpose of causing injury to another person." Thus the antique theory defining ownership as the right to use and to abuse the thing owned is done away with. The increase of discretionary privileges extended to the

[8] "The Civil Code of the Republic of China," translated to English by Hsia, Chow and Chang, published by Hong Kong, Kelly & Walsh, Limited, 1930.

court indicates a substantial advance in the application of human psychology to law.

Doctors never quite know how prevalent certain diseases are because some people never present themselves for treatment. Similarly, the jurist is unable to tell us the size of the criminal population because many criminals are never detected, in the sense of being actually caught and identified, as the individuals who have committed the act which offends society. The causes of crime are, first, matters of human deviation, or abnormality; and, second, times of special stress and emotional excitement in so-called normal individuals. The two general groupings have received the more legal names of predisposing causes and motivating causes. It is perfectly obvious that they are just such things as naturally concern psychology and that "For centuries law has been fumbling with what has only recently become the subject matter of psychology."[9]

The human beings who are likely to be considered criminals or to engage in such behavior as will run counter to society and to law, are the insane, the feeble-minded, drug addicts, and individuals in whom the moral sense and perspective have been decidedly warped by a peculiar environment, such, for example, as the slum areas of a great city. The psychologist holds that people are not born criminals but that sometimes individuals are born into such circumstances as will almost certainly prompt behavior which society will regard as criminal.

The emotional instability often present in a psychopathic personality constitutes an assembled and waiting mechanism, which on slight stimulation may precipitate social distress in one form or another, with the result that this inadequate personality becomes a legal case. Some of the most atrocious crimes have probably been committed

[9] HUTCHINS, R. M., and D. SLESINGER, Legal Psychology, *Psychological Review*, Vol. 36, pp. 13-26, 1929.

by psychopaths. The individual suffering from delusions of persecution is another readily available open keg of gunpowder set to explode from some chance spark. The identification of such personalities by psychiatrists and psychologists and the arranging of their lives in such a way that these calamitous things may not result, is an important service to society.

The feeble-minded criminal is not so capricious as is the insane. He is most typically an individual who has had little education; he wanders from job to job, and may be a vagrant and guilty of thieving, breaking into and entering buildings. He plunges headlong into violence in order to protect himself. The mentally defective criminal is usually guilty simply of offenses in which property is involved, but if caught unawares and afraid of the consequences he may commit crimes against persons also, that is, mayhem or murder. Many studies have been undertaken to determine the amount of feeble-mindedness present in groups of delinquent children and adult criminals. These have recently been ably reviewed by Pintner.[10] The older generalization that about 70 per cent of delinquent children were feeble-minded is not borne out by later studies which place the value nearer 20 per cent. There is general agreement on the low average I. Q. of delinquents. Among adults, delinquent and criminal, several of the more recent surveys indicate the average incidence of feeble-mindedness as about 25 per cent. Much depends on the sample measured; for example, it turns out that the application of the Army Alpha test to more than eight hundred male prisoners in one of the large state prisons shows average results only slightly below those for a large military camp in the same state. There seems, however, to be a much lower per cent of superior intelligence among delinquents than is generally

[10] PINTNER, R., "Intelligence Testing: Methods and Results," New York, Henry Holt & Company, 1931. See Chapter XVI, pp. 374-397.

found for sample non-delinquent groups. Pintner states that "Recidevists test higher than first offenders." These glimpses into the field of mental ability and delinquent behavior indicate substantial contributions from psychology, and point to a fruitful possible cooperation with law.

Another not infrequent cause of crime, over-indulgence in intoxicants, appears to arise from psychologically casting off restraint and giving the more primitive emotional trends free rein. When intoxicants are consistently used for narcotic purposes this tends to indicate a blemish, acute or chronic, in the personality. Individuals who in this manner court unrestrained emotional life cannot be expected suddenly to exhibit normal restraint under those very situations which naturally arouse jealousy and hatred. The narcotic drug is a double-edged predisposing agency making for crime. It has its own effect of making the normal man somewhat like a feeble-minded person and it has also a compelling attraction which prompts the addict to do all sorts of illegal things to gain possession of more of the very substance which is causing his downfall.

Concerning the arousal of emotions in normal people as causes of crime, Moss[11] writes as follows:

In the last analysis the real basis for crime is found in the nature of those who commit crimes. As long as it is human nature to become jealous, and to long for revenge, just so long will murders be committed; and as long as the tendency to become angry is an essential part of the make-up of man, so long will we have crimes of assault and battery. As long as men and women are prone to love not wisely but too well, so long will the eternal triangle exist; and so long as the possession of property can give to its possessor so many of the pleasures of life so long will there

[11] Moss, F. A., "Applications of Psychology," Boston, Houghton Mifflin Company, 1929. See Chapter XV, Psychology and Law, p. 277.

[127]

be injunctions like the following: "Get money, my son, get money. Honestly if you can, dishonestly if you can't, but get money."

A large proportion of the crimes of killing are due to quarrels over petty sums of money, intoxicating liquors, and other drugs, and over sex matters. The emotional and general mental unbalance in the crime situation is indicated by the trifling nature of the things which precipitate the crime-producing disputes; these matters are more subjective than they are objective. They are in the mind of the individual primarily.

Psychology has contributed importantly in the matter of the detection of individual criminals. The basis of detection lies in the impossibility of escaping from one's own individuality. The behavior patterns and habit systems which allow criminal action cannot permanently hide themselves under an appearance of normality. Although the criminal can change his clothing, name, and location he can't change his brains any more than he can alter his finger prints except by doing violence to them. Psychological finger prints are telltale and the new science is working them out. An artist's pictures show similarities. The same principle is true for the writer, banker, and plumber; they can hardly limit themselves to just one production of a kind. The criminal arranges his schemes and does his work along lines preferred by himself; in fact they are himself, they employ just his particular attitudes, interests, prejudices, and special knowledge in a way that is as distinctive as the finger print. To distinguish the behavior trail of one individual from another is simply to follow tracks that differ as much from one another as a cat's do from a rabbit's. Detective agencies, in the spirit and with the viewpoint of modern psychology, were the first to make these applications to the problem of detection. The method really corresponds to the history taking in medicine. There have always been practical psychologists in this field as in the other but it is only with the systematizing of facts by the experimental method that the reliability or unreliability of "hunches" have been definitely determined and the results made available for the entire profession.

Deception tests have also been developed in the psychological laboratory. Apparatus used in tests of this sort is sometimes called a lie-detector. The most generally demonstrated method of lie detection is a modification of the psychological word-association test. If I pronounce the word white a large per cent of my hearers will next think of black. A good many will, however, think house, bread, man, etc. If a person responded with the word money you would be somewhat surprised, which shows that we count on certain mental relationships. Now if you tell a person always to respond with the first word he thinks of after each word that you give (and you record the pairs of words), and if you take the time by stop watch or more exact means from the moment you speak until he speaks, you will get qualitative and quantitative results which can be profitably studied. The association test tends to get at the foreground of consciousness. The fact is that if the individual has something particularly troublesome in mind, which, however, he has no special need to conceal, this material as represented in words is likely to crop out in prompt responses indicative of their psychological setting. If, on the other hand, the individual under test is striving to keep his knowledge secret then he will probably suppress first thoughts because they are incriminatory and he will select later ones that have arisen from them. He can't operate his mind in the usual way on the basis of the confusion which it contains under the criminal conditions. The very prompt responses indicate habitual connections or connections favored by recent or intense experience. On

[129]

examining the responses requiring a very long time interval we usually find odd words such as money for white, indicating that intermediate thoughts have been considered and discarded. If the stimulus words are carefully chosen with reference to two or three concrete situations, only one of which the examinee can have experienced, and if with these are twice as many stimulus words of a neutral character, then it is usually possible to diagnose past circumstances correctly.

After an experiment in which the four people who represented the "criminals" were promptly detected in the presence of a large university class, another student who had witnessed the entire demonstration said he could "beat it," that is, he could go through the test without incriminating himself. He demanded to be tried. He had heard the entire list of stimulus words four times and was fairly aware of the details of the two situations that were being used as incriminating. However, the additional routine was carried through with him as it had been with the others. He was given one of the experiences that constituted the "crime." He endeavored to nullify the laws of mental association by responding to each and every stimulus word in a methodically very slow manner, always allowing some intermediate thoughts before speaking. But he was correctly detected anyway because when he came to the significant words he overplayed his game and took response time that was out of proportion to the rest of his work. Hence these responses stood out from the others and so declared his mental content.

The more recent work on deception has made use of blood-pressure responses accompanying questioning. An apparatus is provided which writes a continuous blood-pressure tracing. A large number of neutral questions are asked and among these are some relating to the crime. When the questioning touches spots that the suspect is anxious to keep dark the average person shows a response in blood pressure, commonly a rise. This may be prompt or it may be somewhat delayed, and so the questions are not put too rapidly.

The application of these techniques requires of course discretion and insight. All details are important and need to be evaluated, as do bullet marks or footprints by a specialist. The tests are not perfect; perhaps no tests can be; human nature is too many-sided. (In no field of human response or behavior are there just two types or kinds, a plus type and a minus type.) But they do have considerable reliability, particularly as compared to the old and still useful method of questioning and cross-examining. Jurists, however, cannot yet look with favor on the new methods, partly because they have generally accepted the principle of free-will agency and have not made mental habit an important matter of evidence. Society is anxious that the courts shall proceed cautiously and not lose any of the insights of the past which have satisfactorily interpreted human nature and aided in adjusting it to community living. Muensterberg's overzealous book, "On the Witness Stand," interfered with the cooperation that might have profitably been undertaken between psychology and law, and which may reasonably come later.

Hutchins and Slesinger, from the standpoint of the law, have brilliantly presented parts of the subject matter of modern psychology that are implied in the techniques and regulations of the courts and used by the law in its various branches. A few examples will serve: the law generally assumes that silence is a manifestation of consent, that evidence of flight tends to show consciousness of guilt, that sworn testimony is more reliable than unsworn, etc. To what extent are these now found to be psychologically sound assumptions? The court will allow the relations between the wife of the victim and the defendant in a

[131]

murder trial to be investigated; it will admit as evidence the spontaneous exclamations of one who has just received a severe physical shock, provided the exclamations are made within a brief period (less than fifteen minutes) after the shock; but in general it will not admit data on the habits of the individual who is being tried. Hutchins and Slesinger ask:

Are these psychological practices? Do men generally say that they do not own property if they do own it? Do men confess to crimes when they are not guilty of them? Do people fabricate business records though the casual observer would think that they were complicating life by doing so? . . . The courts hold that though a man will not lie against his proprietary or pecuniary interest, he may lie if his statement, instead of costing him money, would merely send him to the electric chair. [12]

These problems indicate the great complexity of this field and the desirability of close and sympathetic cooperation between law and psychology.

Law has always had its psychology in its interpretation of human motives and conduct; it had to have assumptions and principles of this kind. In general they have been rough and ready but usually conservative principles and they have worked remarkably well. Psychology, as the modern science of mental life and human behavior, should be able to help clarify certain points about the causes of crime, the personnel of the criminally inclined group, the identification of the offender, preparation of the case for trial and its conduct, and the corrective measures applied and their after effect. Already there have been contributions of importance in connection with the juvenile courts. Apparently some psychological data are near at hand for application elsewhere. And we believe that as social relations tend increasingly toward world social relations, humanity

[12] HUTCHINS and SLESINGER, *ibid*, p. 25.

the more earnestly strives to understand itself thoroughly and to evaluate accurately human motives, behavior, and rights.

Psychology and Theology

In the nature of things, theology, the science of religion, like law and medicine, has within itself the seeds of a psychology founded squarely on human life and its activities. In fact religion is the one of the three from which we expect the achievement of the most thorough, sympathetic, and intimate knowledge of man's mind, and the most complete working out of the principles which govern it. In the doctrines and in the lives of many of the great and wise teachers and preachers of religion throughout the course of world history the practical aspects of the psychology of religion and the religious life have been nobly illustrated often in the simplest and most comprehensible fashion. But in spite of the warnings of these truly wise and good people it has been a peculiar mark of many theological systems that they have presupposed and posited an absolute world order in which religious values as defined by certain individuals hold the uppermost position. All else, including often enough the possibilities of happiness in individuals, has been arranged in rank order below these mystic values and subordinated to them. In theory this system is organized (or revealed) as a means of giving salvation and hope to the individual, but in practice it has too often been made the means of enslaving both mind and body. Thus in the place where the best of all methods and organizations is looked for, men have found from age to age particularly flagrant instances of system versus individual. "They bind on men burdens grievous to be born and lift not so much as a little finger," are ancient words characterizing the activity of some religious systematizers.

[133]

The tendency to institutionalize and to crystallize has thus been so commonly present that religious groups have not made as much progress in the direction of understanding human nature, individual difference, development, adjustment, intellectual life, emotional life, and accomplishment as some of its far-sighted interpreters may have hoped. Those who were prosperous, physically comfortable, and able to fill their lives with agreeable activity and pleasure were apt to lay little stress on religious matters, and so the ministry of the Church has been chiefly a formal one for them. On the other hand it has had to perform active service in comforting the sorrowful, sympathizing with the oppressed, and encouraging those who have lost their courage. Stress upon the sorrows, oppression, and discouragement of mankind, frequent reference to submission, inferiority, and failure, with a compensatory emphasis on freedom of the will have given a rather poor picture of mankind in much religious teaching. In an effort to emphasize the importance of spiritual values religion has sometimes neglected fundamental physical ones. The human body then received too little respect, for it was thought to be so temporary a thing of the dust that its ways and functions did not warrant attention. Happily, in most periods and particularly in the modern era a practical realism has been combined with the mystic idealism of religion. And out of modern religious sentiment we have seen develop some of society's most conspicuous reforms, as illustrated by the revolt against slavery, the substitution of humane for cruel treatment of the insane, and intelligent prison reform.

The religious world has usually been thought of as a double world, that is, a world lying in two planes. One of the two levels, the lower one, was concerned with the needs of the man-to-man relationship, and the other, the higher plane, with the transcendental, the world of permanent values, where compensatory adjustment could be expected for those who suffered at the lower level. The one plane objectifies and idealizes an anthropocentric and faulty world and the other a theocentric and perfect universe. In religious systems generally the latter has been regarded as the one in whose terms life adjustment was to be worked out. In the face of the thwartings, discouragements, prostrating plagues, wars, obvious miscarriages of justice, grievous social complications, and life tragedies, it is no wonder that a system was developed which allowed so heavy an emphasis upon the possibilities which another world outside of this one could offer to poor, suffering, disheartened men and women. But the emphasis upon this other world and its importance was often reflected in the attitudes of its earthly representatives and so the worldly prestige of spiritual officers often resulted. Religion at its best meant a recognition of the importance of fundamental values; at its worst an emphasis upon forms and observances designed to interpret these transcendental experiences. Individual psychology which concerns itself so largely with the development and social reorganization of mental life has had something to say about the facts of the religious life.

The formal side of religious life, an expression chiefly of man's adherence to tradition and social habit, concerns psychology but little. The vital, experiential side, individual recognition of religious values and striving to embody them in daily life, emancipation from the bonds and worries of the physical environment by figuratively lifting oneself on to the higher level, the exchange of worldly values for spiritual values: all these are important matter for psychological study. Briefly, they may be classed for purposes of psychological discussion, under two heads: (1) conversion, the phenomenon of changing one's residence or citizenship while still on this earth from the worldly to the spir-

[135]

itual or heavenly community, (2) the effect of this exchange and its character upon daily activity, in individual experience and in social relations.

In an important big volume, "Varieties of Religious Experience," published just thirty years ago, William James devoted his marvelous abilities to the first part of this problem. The result was a great series of psychological portraits of rather unstable and abnormal personalities and their explosive and spectacular experiences. It was an imposing lot of material that seemed to have in it the homogeneity of the abnormal element. It stressed the behavior tendency, illustrated in religion, of flight from unpleasant reality, and seemed definitely to imply that the inadequately oriented and adjusted individuals who were apt to drop all and flee to religion as their city of refuge were the typical representatives of religion. James's studies were first-rate, well-selected observations and have remained standard until the present. But they are important only as pathological material is important in connection with normal material. Their extreme emphasis was unfortunately forgotten by many readers and they had the effect of stampeding "scientific opinion" toward thinking that all religion and religious experience were just so many symptoms of abnormal mental life.

This discovery of the distinctly psychological factors in some extreme examples of religious experience must be credited to scientific psychology as a significant contribution to the psychology of religion. We can better evaluate it, however, in the light of its historical position and in connection with still other more recent contributions. It was made at a time when the analytic attack was the favored one in psychology. Now when the approach is rather from the standpoint of total personality we see not only that these figures do not tell the whole story for religion but also that this turning of certain abnormal individuals toward religion was the most natural adjustment for them, and therapeutically perhaps the most helpful thing that was to be done in their lives. Through religion these people, many of them remarkably gifted individuals, worked out life integrations where there had formerly been largely conflict and chaos. Through religion they found joy in living and became persons of great social value.

The psychological studies that have been made on emotional manifestations, conversion, stigmata, fear, cures and ascetic tendencies, have perhaps given the general impression that psychology regards religion as chiefly a morbid manifestation. This is far from the truth. Psychology has shown how some unusual mental types have gravitated and continue to gravitate toward certain forms of religious activity and expression. But psychology recognizes religion in the wider sense as a perfectly normal part of human experience and sees in it the most commonly acceptable and satisfying philosophy of life. This brings us to the second contribution of psychology to religion in the analysis of the part which religion may play in normal living.

There is no war between real science and real religion, although it is common for two camps to be formed and regular debates held. Under the rules of this contest two philosophies of life are admitted: the naturalistic and the religious. The position of naturalism may be briefly outlined. It is a pressing forward to discover the relationships of the world and to convert them into a series of mathematically formulated laws. Starting from the discovery that the same stuff which is found in inanimate matter is found also in living organisms, it proceeds to discover that the forces of physics and chemistry also determine the course of life processes. Another step was made when the relationship between the course of mental experience and the physio-

[137]

logical brain processes was found. Then came the theory of evolution which placed man in relation to the rest of the living world, gave him a position in the series of creatures, and showed his essential and direct connection with the total scheme of nature. For naturalism, proceding from these premises, the same laws which hold everywhere else in nature hold also for man—and only these laws hold.

The religious philosophy of life, in contrast to the foregoing position, points out that a world whose laws may be thoroughly known still remains a mystery. It states that the knowledge that laws govern the universe by no means precludes the possibility that the world may be conditioned by other factors as well and dependent on them also. The religious point of view proposes that even through the most complete scientific study we do not and cannot grasp the true essence and depth of phenomena; that the world that we perceive is only the appearance of the true essence of things and that we only touch on the true essence in our guesses and yearnings. Although natural science with all its tremendous development and advance can as yet say nothing about the final purpose in the world, religion holds that this does not mean that ideals and purposes are not present and that a providence in the conduct of affairs does not exist. Religion emphasizes that faith in higher realities by no means hinders the systematic procedure in studying nature but rather that it may further it. The mystery of the world, higher realities than those perceived through the separate senses, and some kind of ultimate and transcendant power: these are the contributions of religion to science which the religious debaters stress. Psychology is both the logical and the practical go-between for these two camps and as the currents of discussion are now moving it will probably in time unite the two points of view and so release activity for some other more profitable purpose than that of debate. This is a bold statement but made quite sincerely.

Recent psychological study (observation in psychiatry and mental hygiene) indicates that a religious philosophy of life is apt to offer most people a more favorable basis for personality adjustment and development than any other. It shows that the teaching and developing of those characteristics and values which religion emphasizes when combined with recognition and knowledge of the laws of the scientific universe offer the best introduction to living at the highest human level. A balanced philosophy of life which renders to religion the things that are religious and to science the things that belong to science has the best chance of making complete and happy personalities, those that are best able to meet life's problems and help others to meet them.

The normal human life is built on factors which make for unity and continuity. The life processes take place in a body that has individuality and persists much the same from decade to decade. Habits are formed and memories registered in the mind which continue as real features of the personality. Likes and dislikes, temperamental trends and special abilities are not short lived to be annexed or exchanged at will. Care of the physical organism by medicine, protection of the social relationships by law, development of a sense of values through religion, integration of all these services through the psychology that is in them and through psychology as a specialty—these are the cooperative objectives of the professions today.

Turning from medicine, law, and theology as professional entities let us consider the psychology of a concrete individual.[13] A young man of eighth-grade education and normal intelligence enlisted in the army at the age of sixteen. After being transferred to two camps he one day had an attack of paralysis that involved his entire left side. This came to

[13] TRAVIS, R. C., A Study of the Effect of Hypnosis on a Case of Dissociation Precipitated by Migraine, *American Journal of Psychology*, Vol. 36, pp. 207–213, 1925.

him on the drill field. He suddenly fell to the ground in a sort of faint and was unconscious for a short time. He could move none of the muscles of his left side, nor could he feel any contact with that side except through the skin of the face and neck. He was given the best of medical attention over a period of about two months, during which there was little change. Then the medical officers decided to send him to Plattsburg for electrical therapy. The young man on hearing this began to improve immediately and within two days his entire left side began to tingle and he found he was able to walk about, although his leg and arm seemed rather stiff.

During the next seven years this young man's general bodily health was fair but he had seven periods of striking mental discontinuity. Just before one of these he would leave the camp in uniform as usual. Then would come a blank and two months later he would come back to himself in some distant city. How he had arrived there, or why, he did not know. The seventh lapse of this sort occurred after the young man had enlisted in the Marine Corps. He had worked up to the position of first-class private and was apparently enjoying his work immensely. Suddenly one day he felt a severe headache. He went a short distance to the "sick barracks" to get something to relieve the headache, and this was the last he remembered in his normal state. But in the strange lapsed condition he went from the camp to Washington, traveled thence from city to city, through eastern and central states, beating his way. He trained himself as an expert window cleaner and followed this occupation when remaining in a city for any length of time. Finally after four months of wandering he came back to his normal consciousness in Windsor, Canada. He had a strange feeling that he was lost. He immediately oriented himself as to time and place, and mailed a card to his mother saying he would be home very soon. When he came home

child and adult psychology; the possibilities for good or evil in the powerful sex drive; practical classifications of personality types. The clinics, courts and sanctuaries of the future, like those of the past, will have their psychologists, but we believe generally more effective ones because more specifically trained and made responsible for particular phases of human life which are now clearly in view. And through cooperation with their colleagues in research and practice there should come much human gain. Large medical centers are in the present decade organizing cooperative programs to facilitate these ends. Law schools are organizing clinics to give their students practical experience and the public legal aid; and ministers are establishing the "life adjustment center" a new kind of multiple-expert clinic that draws upon all the professions, the psychologist, and the business executive, to aid in identifying and adjusting those features of personal and social living which interfere with abundant life.

Chapter VI

PSYCHOLOGY AND INDUSTRY

by Morris S. Viteles[1]

Human reactions—of man to man, of man to machine and material—occupy a prominent place in the complex pattern of industrial enterprise. Underlying every industrial process, as mechanized as it may be, and often closely associated with it, are human ingenuity and control. The accomplishments of an industrial organization are circumscribed by the human element—by the capacity for organization of its leaders, the skill of its working personnel, the clash of motivation between its management and its workers. The stability of business enterprise depends no less upon the soundness of its psychological foundations than upon the solidity of its economic and technical supports.

It was the recognition of the importance of the human factor in the effectiveness of industrial organization that led Edison to predict that "problems in human engineering will receive during the coming years the same genius and attention which the nineteenth century gave to the more material forms of engineering." Psychology as applied in industry represents an expression of the concern for individual welfare implied in this statement.

[1] The writer is Assistant Professor of Psychology at the University of Pennsylvania. He has had wide industrial experience as consulting psychologist with a number of public utilities and manufacturing plants. As Director of Personnel Research in the Philadelphia Electric Company, he is administering an extensive program involving the application of psychological methods in promoting the adjustment and efficiency of workers employed by this organization. He is preparing for early publication a volume on industrial psychology.

[144]

In its application in other fields, psychology is not altogether a new science. As many as forty years ago, experiments were made in the measurement of the intelligence of college students by means of psychological tests. For the last thirty-five years, the examination of children by means of psychological tests, for the purpose of determining degrees of educability and for clearing up problems of juvenile delinquency, has been carried on regularly in psychological clinics throughout the country. As a matter of fact, even in industry the application of psychology is not altogether new, for, as many as twenty years ago, Dr. Muensterberg, of the Psychological Laboratory of Harvard, undertook investigations intended to develop tests for the selection of workers for industry and to promote the application to business, in other ways, of the knowledge which the psychologist possesses about human behavior. It is, however, only within the last few years, gaining impetus from the demands for increased industrial efficiency arising during the war, that the greatest strides have been made in the application of this science in business.

In its applications in industry, psychology seeks to satisfy two objectives.

The first is to promote the adjustment of the worker—to insure a high degree of satisfaction from his work.

The second is to increase industrial efficiency—to decrease the cost of production, cost of accidents, and of other larger expense items in the budget of the industrial concern.

Adjustment of the Individual Worker

The effect upon the individual of maladjustment in work cannot be overemphasized. Excessive fatigue, excessive irritation, a complete loss of emotional balance may result from an attempt on the part of the worker to continue on a job for which he is not adapted. These effects are displayed not only in the factory—in his production, in his contacts

[145]

with his fellow workers and supervisors—but they may be carried into the home. When carried into the home, they may result in conflict between husband and wife, and in misunderstanding between father and children. Maladjustments in every aspect of an individual's life may follow from lack of proper adjustment to his job.

The worker on the wrong job suffers not only difficulties in social adjustment; he suffers from reduced earnings; he suffers from the probability of increased accidents and from many other similarly direct handicaps leading to the creation of a vicious circle of "misfortunes" from which he cannot extricate himself.

The complexity of this condition may be so great and the maladjustment so severe as to lead to a pathological disintegration of personality. The relationship between mild psychopathic disorder and maladjustment in industry finds striking confirmation in the recent findings of Smith and Culpin[2] on the heightened degree of susceptibility to telegraphist's cramp of incompetent neurotics in this occupation. Frequently men have been heard to say, "I'll go crazy if I stick to this job much longer." Actually men have developed insanities by reason of maladjustment to the job. Many years ago Janet, a French psychologist, and Wetterkampf, a German, pointed out the incidence of vocational maladjustments among patients in hospitals for the insane.

The cost of maladjustment in industry falls not only upon the individual but upon the industry as well. In the transportation industry alone, the cost of accidents which can be avoided by the elimination of accident-prone operators amounts to millions. The street railway company of Paris,[3]

[2] SMITH, M., and CULPIN, M. A Study of Telegraphist's Cramp, *Industrial Fatigue Research Board*, *Report* 43, 40 pp., London, 1927.

[3] LAHY, J. M., "La Selection psychophysiologique des travailleurs, conducteurs de tramways et d'autobus," 227 pp., Paris, Dunod, 1927.

for example, reports an annual saving of over 1,300,000 francs through an application of psychological techniques in the selection of accident-free motor-vehicle operators. The cost to industry and the general social effects of incompetent or maladjusted workers can be readily illustrated in the case of electrical substation operation. Economy in the distribution of electric current involves generation and transmission at high voltages which are reduced at electrical substations prior to the delivery of current to the consumer. The substation is supplied with a number of lines through which current is received from generating stations, and with a greater number of circuits through which the current at a lower voltage is transferred directly to individual consumers or to equipment through which several consumers may be served. Associated with the lines and the circuits are a great variety of equipment for transforming and regulating voltages, a great number of recording meters, relaying and other protective devices, rotative equipment, etc. The operation of this equipment involves the manipulation of numerous switches. The operator at such substations is responsible for the manipulation of switches, the reading of meters, and the care of the station and its equipment in such a manner as to provide regular and uninterrupted service to the consumer.[4]

The importance of maintaining uninterrupted service is almost self-evident. A brief reference to the possible effects of an interruption following upon the inaccurate operation of switches may serve to demonstrate more clearly the significance of methods of selection and training, etc., through which the number of operating errors may be reduced. If, for example, an interrupted circuit is feeding a hospital, serious consequences may follow from unexpected failure of lights or power equipment, particu-

[4] VITELES, M. S., The Human Factor in Substation Operation, *The Personnel Journal*, Vol. 8, pp. 81–113, 1929.

larly if an operation is being performed at the time. There are industrial operations in which even a momentary interruption may cause serious damage to material in the process of manufacture. So, for instance, in the manufacture of rayon the failure of the supply of power to machines causes a break in the manufacturing process involving considerable loss to the manufacturing concern. It has been estimated that the actual cost of even a momentary interruption in one such plant is $6,000. The entire load of a grain elevator may be dumped upon the operating motor if the current is interrupted for even a fraction of a minute. In addition to such inconveniences and losses, and to possible damage to very expensive equipment in the substation itself, there may be more serious consequences of an operating error in the form of injury to the operator or of actual loss of life. This is especially apt to be the case when the man undertakes to handle as "dead," equipment which is actually alive. Mechanical and electrical safeguards against such occurrences are provided, but these cannot completely take the place of human control exercised by an operator, physically and mentally competent, and prepared by suitable training to handle the job.

The cost of spoiled work in manufacturing and of increases in production time are additional items of cost to industry in particular, and to society in general, of individual maladjustment in industry.

The Selection of Workers

There are a number of ways in which psychology is employed in furthering the objectives of promoting individual happiness and efficiency in industry. The first of these takes the form of a scientific selection of workers.

Every job has two aspects:

a. *The work to be done;*
b. *The man who is to do it.*

Unless there is proper dovetailing between these two aspects there can be neither efficiency in production nor, what is of still greater importance, happiness and contentment on the part of the man who is doing the job.

Selective adjustment of workers at the time of employment is one of the best ways of promoting the happiness of the worker and of insuring his efficiency and welfare, especially in an organization in which there are many jobs to which he can be fitted. For new workers it is a means of avoiding unnecessary transfer from job to job, from plant to plant, and the heartbreaking disappointment which comes from not making good on a job after a trial period of service. To workers already employed on a job, especially in a hazardous occupation, it is comforting to know that the men placed alongside of them are of such caliber that they will not, by reason of incompetence, contribute further to hazards inherent in the job. From the viewpoint of the management the contribution of scientific selection toward the increase of productive efficiency and toward the reduction of production, accident, and allied costs is in itself sufficient justification for the introduction of such procedures.

The Nature of Individual Differences

The employment of scientific techniques in the selection of workers involves an application in the industrial situation of the principle of individual differences. This principle is merely a recognition of the fact that, in spite of what has been said about men being free and equal, there are no such things as equality of ability or of exact similarity in temperament. One of the most characteristic things about human nature is its variability, the extent to which one individual differs from another.

The nature and range of individual differences in mental traits have been submitted to very careful study in the psychological laboratory. The character of the traits

[149]

examined and the range of differences can be easily illustrated by reference to the findings with respect to one of the most important of the mental traits—*memory span*.

The measure of memory span is the number of units which the individual can associate in one moment of consciousness. For example, an examiner reads off, under standard conditions; a series of digits—5, 1, 6, 9, 2. Anyone who can reproduce this series in the correct order immediately after its presentation is said to have a memory span of at least five. If he can reproduce as many as eight, he is said to have a memory span of eight. An examination of thousands of individuals has shown that there are some individuals who cannot reproduce more than two digits, who in other words have a memory span of no more than two, whereas there are others whose memory span is as high as thirteen.

The range of memory span would have no significance if differences in this trait were not associated with very definite accomplishments in the workaday world. So, for example, the very low memory span of two, in adults, is generally associated with feeble-mindedness. It apparently requires, among other things, the ability to keep more than two things in mind at the same time to adjust oneself to the complex conditions of life existing outside of an institution for the feeble-minded.

A memory span of at least three is necessary for the acquisition of the equivalent of a fifth-grade education. In addition, in the case of the many thousands of college students who have been examined, we have not yet found a college student with a memory span of less than five. Moreover, college students with memory spans of only five generally exhibit marked deficiency in their academic achievements. The average memory span of the college student is eight.

Not only in academic achievement but also in the industrial situation, memory span appears to be of great importance. So, for example, in the case of the street-car motorman and automobile driver the capacity to associate or hold in his mind a number of discrete stimuli is an important factor in the safety of operation. In many other occupations involving a distribution of attention over a variety of stimulating conditions, differences in the length of the memory span assume great importance.

Another trait may be employed to illustrate the nature of individual differences, their range, their significance, and the techniques employed in their investigation. This is a trait known as *reaction time*. It represents the time elapsing between the appearance of a stimulus and the response to it. In the psychological laboratory, this time is measured in terms of one thousandth of a second. In an experiment by Moss and Allen[5] on automobile drivers, a range of from 0.31 second to 1.02 seconds in the time taken to apply the brake in response to an auditory stimulus was observed, the average reaction time being .54 seconds. When it is recalled that an automobile traveling at the rate of 25 miles per hour covers approximately 35 feet per second, the significance of an individual difference in reaction time of .31 second in one case and 1.02 seconds in another appears enormous. As a matter of fact, this difference in reaction time between two individuals may lead to a serious accident on the part of the one with the longer reaction time in a situation which brings no danger to the individual who can start applying the brake 0.3 second after he has heard a disturbing noise.

A number of investigators, including Förster,[6] stress reaction time as the most important factor in safe driving

[5] Moss, F. A., and H. H. ALLEN, The Personal Equation in Automobile Driving, *Journal of the Society of Automotive Engineers*, Vol. 16, pp. 415–420, 1925.

[6] FÖRSTER, W. A., Test for Drivers, *The Personnel Journal*, Vol. 7, pp. 161–171, 1928.

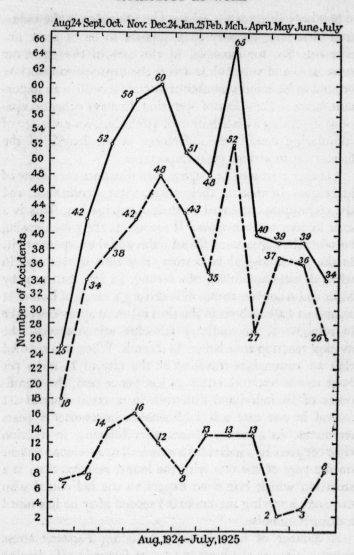

Fig. 1.—Accidents involving railroad employees. (*After Schmitt, E., Unfallaffinität und Psychotechnik im Eisenbahndienst, Industrielle Psychotechnik, Vol. 3, pp. 363–366, 1926.*)

and in other industrial situations. The evidence is somewhat contradictory, but it is worth consideration.

The significance of individual differences has also been shown in the analysis of causes of accidents in industry. Every analysis has shown that

. . . accidents do not distribute themselves by chance, but they happen frequently to some men and infrequently to others as a logical result of a combination of circumstances. Those individuals who because of certain mental or physical defects fail to control a situation leading to an accident when it arises, usually become involved, while those possessing the necessary physical and mental requirements show little susceptibility to accidents.[7]

This susceptibility to accident has come to be termed accident proneness. The existence of accident proneness is very well illustrated in Fig. 1 showing the number of accidents sustained during a year by railroad employees who had previously been *involved in only one accident* as compared with those who had already been *involved in more than one accident.*

Of the total number of accidents, the first group is responsible for only 21.2 per cent, whereas 78.2 per cent of the accidents are sustained by men who have already been involved in more than one accident, in spite of the fact that the latter constitute the smaller group.

The existence of such accident proneness has been demonstrated in many studies of street-car operation, in which it is invariably discovered that a relatively small group of motormen is responsible for a large percentage of accidents although operating under identical conditions with the larger group of motormen whose accident records are good.

[7] The Accident Prone Employee, A Study of Electric Railway Operation undertaken by The Cleveland Railway Company, with the co-operation of Policyholders' Service Bureau, Metropolitan Life Insurance Company, 26 pp., New York, 1930.

The Measurement of Individual Differences in Selecting Workers

The basic problem in promoting vocational adjustment and industrial efficiency through the scientific selection of workers is to select those men who are superior in the traits or behavior patterns which are required for successful

FIG. 2.—Viteles Motormen Selection Test (New Model, 1925).

work on the job. A number of techniques have been employed by psychologists in measuring aptitudes for various kinds of jobs. The technique which is most frequently employed is that of the psychological test.

It is impossible here to describe in detail the steps which must be taken in the experimental analysis of the qualifica-

[154]

tions for the job and in evaluating tests in the preparation of these scientific, objective measures of vocational aptitude. It is sufficient merely to point out that the tests must be most carefully prepared and that they must be subjected to the most searching analysis to determine their validity before they may be employed in the selection of workers as an aid in the promotion of individual adjustment and efficiency. However, the usefulness of such tests when carefully prepared, standardized, and validated has been demonstrated in more than one experimental investigation,

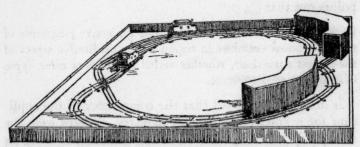

FIG. 3.—Viteles Motormen Selection Test. Close-up view of device used in measuring perception of speed and distance of moving object.

and practical results have been obtained from their use in a variety of industrial situations.

The nature of apparatus which may be employed for testing is shown in Figs. 2 and 3. In connection with these figures, it seems desirable to point out that the psychologist who uses tests does not depend exclusively upon the objective score on the psychological test. He takes into consideration many other pertinent factors. He has been criticized in certain quarters for his willingness to use psychological test scores alone in predicting the adjustment and efficiency of a worker on a job. Where he does so, such criticism is entirely justified.

Psychologists who are interested in the examination of children for educational purposes, for correctional purposes,

[155]

or for purposes of guidance have found it impossible to diagnose and treat on the basis of objective test scores alone. It has been found necessary to supplement the objective data of mental measurement with the observation and analysis of performance. Mental ages, I. Q.'s, and time scores have been found to be useful in guiding the examiner, but not in directly indicating the intellectual level or specific abilities of children.

There is a qualitative aspect of mental analysis which goes hand in hand with quantitative analysis. Maxfield[8] points out that

In the use of standardized mental tests subjective judgments of the experienced examiner in regard to the qualitative aspect of the subject's reactions, whether verbal responses or other types of behavior, are significant.

It must be recognized that the competency of the applicant for a great many jobs in industry, perhaps even for a majority of them, cannot be wholly predicted from an objective score any more than the ability of a child to profit from one or another kind of educational treatment can be wholly gauged from such a score. There is no reason for suspecting that the capacity of an individual motorman to avoid accidents, or of a printer's apprentice to profit from instruction in this trade can be expressed in an objective score, as easily interpreted by a minor clerk as by a trained psychologist, than for suspecting that the mental status of a child is revealed in the I. Q. which can be obtained by any teacher who owns a copy of Terman's "Condensed Guide" and a set of testing material. The one problem is as complicated as the other; the objective score in one case has in it as many elements of error as in the other, and an adequate diagnosis in both involves

[8] MAXFIELD, F. N., The Use and Abuse of Standard Intelligence Tests in Individual Examinations, *Proceedings Forty-eighth Annual Session for the Study of the Feeble-minded*, 1924.

interpretation by a trained psychologist based on observation of performance and a consideration of related data.

The character of such an analysis is illustrated in Fig. 4, which shows the possibilities in the way of a qualitative analysis of the character of performance on an early model of the Viteles Motormen Selection Test shown in Fig. 2.

In the application of the electrical substation operator tests, a great deal of attention is paid to the shape of the curve as well as to the objective score. It has been discovered, for example, that regardless of the objective total test score, operators whose paper test scores are higher than

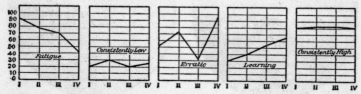

Fig. 4.—*Analysis of motormen test record indicates characteristic tendencies.* (*After Shellow.*) Each curve represents six minutes of performance on the Motormen Selection Test. For example, the average score for the first curve is high but the shape of this curve indicates a rapid fatiguability which must be considered in selection and carefully checked in the training period, if this operator is selected. The shape of the third curve indicates erratic, jumpy qualities in performance, which may be highly significant in operation. (*Dewhurst, J. A., Personnel Selected, and Trained in Milwaukee on Scientific Basis, Electric Railway Journal, Vol.* 67, *pp.* 624–629, 1926.)

their performance scores are generally the least satisfactory. In addition, an analysis of the regularity and irregularity of the curve has suggested that there exists a definite relationship between the degree of irregularity in the curve and the performance and general stability of the operator.

The psychologist also recognizes that the psychological test results, whether considered qualitatively or quantitatively, cannot be considered as the sole or final selection agent. He recognizes that

The interview if properly conducted and intelligently interpreted, opens up knowledge concerning the applicant's past history and ways of behavior that furnishes a most fruitful basis for judging what his future adjustments are likely to be.[9]

However, the psychologist insists upon an objective treatment of the interview, and upon restraint in the formulation of rationalizations and subjective judgments so characteristic of the interview as conducted by the

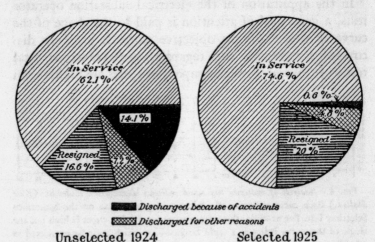

Discharged because of accidents
Discharged for other reasons

Unselected 1924   Selected 1925

Fig. 5.—Tangible results of scientific methods in the selection of motormen. (*After Shellow.*)

archcritic of the psychologist—the psychiatrist. But space prohibits discussion of this problem here.

Figures 5 and 6 illustrate tangible results following from the employment of scientific methods in the selection of workers. The two diagrams in Fig. 5 show the accomplishments made through the scientific selection of motormen on the payroll of the Milwaukee Electric Railway and Light Co.[10]

[9] ANDERSON, V. V., A Psychiatric Guide for Employment, *The Personnel Journal*, Vol. 6, pp. 417-441, 1928.

[10] DEWHURST, J. A., Personnel Selected and Trained in Milwaukee on Scientific Basis, *Electric Railway Journal*, Vol. 67, pp. 624-629, 1926.

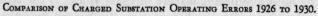

COMPARISON OF CHARGED SUBSTATION OPERATING ERRORS 1926 TO 1930.

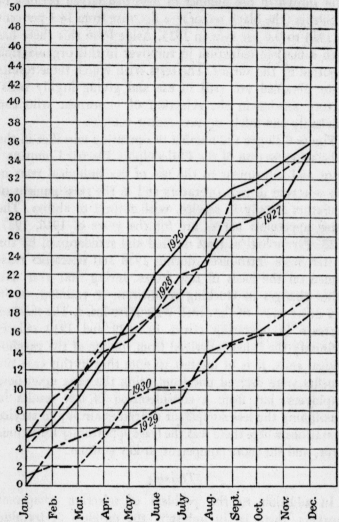

FIG. 6.—Reduction of operating mistakes on part of substation operators employed by Philadelphia Electric Company following introduction of psychological tests. (*After Viteles.*)

The most significant feature of these charts is the reduction shown in the number of men discharged because of accidents (the black sector)—a decrease from 14.1 per cent in 1924 to 0.6 per cent in 1925. Aside from this there has been a marked reduction in turnover in this organization reported by the author. The tests with which these results were obtained are still in use and giving highly satisfactory service in the selection of motormen who can efficiently and safely operate motor vehicles.

Figure 6 shows the number of operating mistakes in the Substation Section of the Philadelphia Electric Company[11] prior and subsequent to the use of psychological tests in the selection of new operators and in the reassignment of operators already in service, with respect to ability. The three uppermost curves are for the years of 1926, 1927, 1928. Psychological tests devised and standardized by the writer were introduced during 1928 and operators reassigned on the basis of test scores during that year. No other changes in working conditions, in training, or in any other items of the work were introduced. The marked decrease in operating errors in 1929 and 1930 reflects definitely the benefits derived from the use of the psychological tests. It is of interest to note that in this case the benefits were derived not from using the tests upon new employees, but from a consideration of test results in reassigning the less competent operators already in service to stations where there was the least opportunity for serious error, and the more competent to key stations.

Training

In addition to the problem of selecting competent workers, there is, in industry, the problem of training individuals selected for given jobs. It must be clearly

[11] VITELES, M. S., The Human Factor in Substation Operation, U. G. I. *Circle*, August, 1930.

recognized that the ultimate proficiency of a worker depends not only upon selection but also upon the proper training of the new worker. A competent applicant may become a very unsatisfactory worker because he has not been properly trained. The recognition of the importance of training in maintaining an efficient working force is leading industry to substitute for the old methods of training, in which the instruction of the worker was largely left to the caprice of the foreman or of some other minor official, a more scientific method, in which instruction is centralized in the hands of a corps especially fitted for the task of training workers. The general phases of the movement for the scientific training of workers in industry cannot be discussed at length here. It is the purpose of this paper merely to point out contributions which psychology makes to the solution of the practical problem of properly training workers in industry. In pointing out these contributions, it is possible merely to cite a few specific instances rather than to develop logically and in detail the psychology of learning.

An important finding of psychological investigations in the laboratory and in the industrial plant is that the acquisition of skill follows a simple, regular course. If the production or achievement of the individual is plotted at various intervals in the learning period, there will develop a curve which is typical of practically every kind of activity. The character of this curve is illustrated in Fig. 7 showing the improvement in telegraphy over a 32-week period in a classic experiment by Bryan and Harter.[12] That the general shape of the curve does not change with the type of activity, is illustrated in Fig. 8 showing the improvement of typewriting by the sight method, from a report on experiments in this field by

[12] BRYAN, W. L. and N. HARTER, Studies in the Physiology and Psychology of the Telegraphic Language, *The Psychological Review*, Vol. 4.

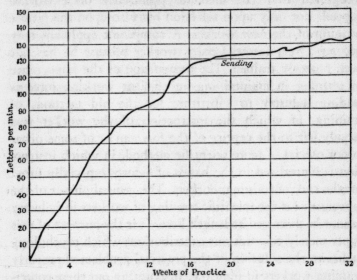

FIG. 7.—Typical practice curve; improvement of W. J. R. in telegraphy. (*After Bryan and Harter.*)

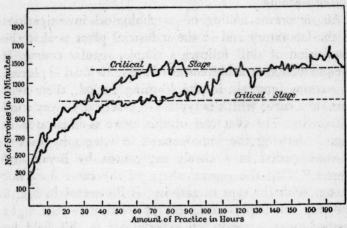

FIG. 8.—Improvement made in typewriting by the sight method. (*After Book.*)

Book.[13] The characteristic features of the practice curve are:—

a. The improvement in work with practice, shown by the rise of the curve to the right;

b. The relatively rapid improvement at the beginning of the learning period as compared with the later period of learning; and

c. The leveling off after practice has been carried on over a period of time.

The leveling off is known as the *plateau level* and represents the point at which the individual settles down to a relatively constant productive rate. Often this occurs at the first plateau level, but experiments have shown that under certain conditions, additional spurts in learning lead to settling at higher plateau levels. In other words, proficiency levels can be raised by changes in training methods, by changes in systems of wage payment, or even by the mere procedure of keeping workers informed of their progress in the acquisition of skill.

Properly employed, such practice curves, maintained for workers during the training period, can be invaluable aids in promoting the effectiveness of instruction. In the first place, they constitute exact records of progress. Proper guidance at the plateau levels can do much toward increasing proficiency, toward discouraging the fixing of production at a level of low efficiency. The effect of changes in methods of work, or of financial and non-financial incentives, can be directly interpreted by the changes appearing in the practice curves of workers subsequent to the introduction of these changes.

In addition, there is evidence which suggests that the progress of a worker at an advanced period of training can be predicted from the character of his work or practice

[13] Book, W. F., "Learning to Typewrite," pp. XVII, 463, New York, Gregg, 1925.

curve during the early period of training. In general, those who start at a low level of production on a new job do not reach the same level of production after a period of training achieved by those who start at a higher level. However, there are many exceptions to this general rule and many conditions influencing the acquisition of skill which make it impossible to formulate a general conclusion for the prediction of the second half of the practice curve from the first. These disturbing conditions make it necessary to resort to an analysis of individual work curves as a means of predicting adjustment to the job. However, the observation of such practice curves, of plotted records of quality and quantity of production, possesses, according to many investigators, high value in predicting the success of workers. The importance of this for apprentice training and for any other skilled work involving long periods of training is self-evident. As a matter of fact, the analysis of practice curves as an aid in adjusting workers and in increasing plant efficiency is considered far superior to psychological tests of the analytical type, of short duration, by Poppelreuter,[14] Sollier and Drabs[15] and many other careful investigators.

The significance of the early training period for prediction has been, perhaps, most strongly urged by Poppelreuter, who stresses the unsuitability of a short test in the determination of vocational aptitude, and insists upon the need of studying individual work or practice curves in determining suitability for a job. He points out that there are apprentices who first work slowly and accurately, but who, after a lapse of time, show a characteristic trend in the direction of fast but inaccurate work. On the other

[14] POPPELREUTER, W., Die Arbeitskurve in der Diagnostik von Arbeitstypen, *Psychotechnische Zeitschrift*, Vol. 3, pp. 35–51, 1928.

[15] SOLLIER, P., and J. DRABS, La Prevision de la perfectabilité des aptitudes motrices, *Revue de la Société du Travail*, Vol. 1, pp. 26–40; 523–538, 1929.

hand, he finds apprentices who, although appearing to be unsatisfactory workers at first, slowly, but with a *high* degree of certainty, develop into satisfactory workers from the viewpoints both of quality and quantity of production. A few typical curves may serve to illustrate these findings.

In Fig. 9 are shown the production records of two subjects on a task involving heavy bodily work of a type that a machinist working on large equipment may be called upon to perform. The character of the work is illustrated in Fig. 10. The subject is instructed to set his own pace, to pause whenever he chooses, to sit down whenever he chooses, etc., and an accurate record is automatically kept of his work.

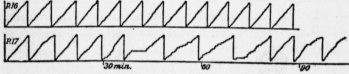

FIG. 9.—Individual practice curves. (*After Poppelreuter.*)

It is easy to observe that the production of the two subjects, P-16 and P-17, is at first about equal. As a matter of fact, the former does not do as well as the latter at first, because he performs the work of lifting the weight to punch the moving band with less regularity. However, with continued practice in the work, there develops greater and greater difference between P-16 and P-17, with the latter exhibiting a consistently irregular and lowered production, characterized by many pauses in work. These characteristics appear only after he has been given an opportunity to engage in the work for a period of time. In this case, their existence could not have been foreseen in the early part of the work period. However, as work curves for longer periods of time are studied, characteristic work traits, of such great importance in training and in final adjustment, are revealed.

[165]

Fig. 10.—Apparatus employed in studying practice curves. (*After Poppelreuter.*)

Although these work curves represent tasks performed in the laboratory rather than in industry, they are characteristic of the type of curves which can be found if the progress of apprentices on objective tasks is followed. The latter procedure permits an even more accurate diagnosis of the work tendencies, a more accurate prediction of the potential proficiency of the apprentices.

The Effect of Habit Interference.—In the training of the motorman[16] may be found another example of the application of principles formulated by experimental psychology in training for practical work in industry. The degree of safety with which a motorman runs a trolley car depends upon the strength of certain habits of response which he forms during his training period. He must learn to use the controller, to use the air-brake lever, to coordinate his response with the controller with those of the air-brake lever, with the bell plunger, the crank for opening the door, etc. The purpose of devoting a period of two or three weeks to training the motorman is to teach him these responses. He must learn these responses so well that when he goes out on the road alone, in full charge of a street car, he performs them without the intervention of consciousness, that is, without thinking, "Now I must turn this handle this way, and step on the plunger," etc., when a given situation arises. The responses, the habits, must be so well established that each stimulus, whether it be a child crossing the track, the sound of the conductor's bell, or the sight of an overhead circuit breaker, will bring at once the appropriate and correct response, the proper series of movements properly coordinated.

The usual procedure adopted by the majority of street railway companies in training motormen is somewhat as follows: The apprentice spends a half day or a day in a

[16] VITELES, M. S., Application of Psychology in Training Workers, *Lefax*, pp. 29–36, 1923.

schoolroom, ordinarily an old car fitted up for this purpose. Here he is taught the simple operations of starting and stopping a car, the meanings of signals, the uses and locations of fuses, the use of the fender, and similar details of operation. He is then assigned to a "run" with a motorman who has been specially chosen, by reason of his record, for the instruction of apprentices. He spends a day with the motorman, watching him run the car and running the car himself under the direction of the motorman. For a period of ten

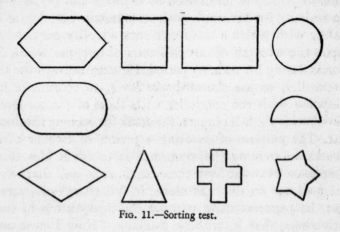

Fig. 11.—Sorting test.

days to two weeks this procedure is continued, the apprentice being assigned each day to a different motorman, on a different run. The purpose in placing the apprentice with the different motormen is to give him contact with a number of experienced, trusted men, from whose example he may profit, and at the same time to enable him to learn something about the different routes, the special difficulties of each, etc. The effect of assigning the new man to different motormen each day in this way is, however, from the point of view of the psychologist, often most harmful. The psychological principles which lead to this conclusion can perhaps best be presented in the analysis of a simple psychological experiment often performed in the psychological laboratory.

In this experiment, known as the Sorting Experiment, are illustrated the *laws of habit formation*, and it is these laws which are violated, as will be pointed out below, in the type of training discussed above. The purpose of the experiment is simply to sort, as quickly as possible, a set of one hundred cards with ten designs similar to those illustrated in Fig. 11. The cards are so shuffled that in no case do two cards with the same design come together. They are sorted to a card, approximately fifteen by twenty inches, placed before the experimenter, upon which the ten designs have been drawn in two rows of five each. Ten trials are made in sorting the cards.

When the results of the ten trials are charted, a curve similar in design to the one shown in Fig. 12*a* is obtained; in other words, a typical practice curve is obtained. The curve slopes downward because units of time instead of production are recorded.

Interference in Habit Formation.—After the cards have been sorted to one order ten times, the experiment is continued. For the card in front of the experimenter another is substituted, upon which the order of the arrangement of the designs has been changed. There are still two rows of five designs each, but some of the designs which were on the first row on the first card are on the second row on the second card, and vice versa. In no case is the same design found in the same position on the two cards. Ten trials are made with this changed order. The curve showing the time taken for the second series of ten trials is shown in Fig. 12*b*. A comparison of Figs. 12*a* and 12*b* shows clearly what generally takes place. During the first three trials with the changed arrangement of the designs on the card to which the experimenter is sorting, the time taken to

[169]

sort the cards is longer than the time for the first three trials of sorting with the first arrangement, when the process of sorting cards to a given order was first being learned. Practically every time this experiment is tried the sorting

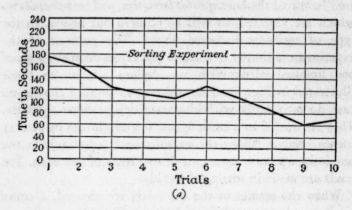

(a)

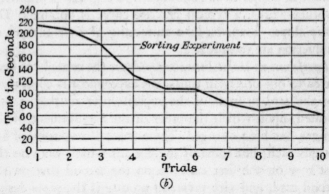

(b)

FIG. 12.—Practice with the sorting test. (*After Viteles.*) Figures on "time in seconds," given in the curves are not actual but hypothetical, approximating those generally obtained by averaging the results of a number of experimenters.

time for the first two or three trials with the changed order is longer than the time in the first two or three trials of the first series. The time then generally decreases, as in the case of the ten trials in the first series until at the end

[170]

of the tenth trial in the second series the time may be less than for the tenth trial in the first series.

It is the first few trials of the two series which interest us here, for we have illustrated in the increase of time for these trials in the second series what is known as *habit interference*. This, and other careful experiments show that when the opposing associations are alternately practiced, they have an interference effect upon each other, particularly during the early practice period. In other words, the formation of a habit is interfered with if other responses, antagonistic to the one being learned, are practiced along with it. The formation of a habit may also be interfered with by one already established. In the first stages of learning to use the typewriter, for example, it is easier for one who has never used a typewriter to learn to use it correctly than one who has already used it, but incorrectly—that is, with one or two fingers or with some similar amateur method.

Application in the Training of Motormen.—In the method of training motormen described above, the law of habit interference is, in practice, generally overlooked. It was found by the author, who learned to run a street car as a step preliminary to the preparation of a test for the selection of motormen, that practically each of the motormen under whom he took training had his special tricks, individual ways of handling the controller and the air-brake handle. Instead of receiving from day to day uniform training in a definite series of responses involving the same muscular combinations, there were changes from day to day. For handling the air brake, for example, one motorman recommended taking "long bites" of air, another recommended "short bites." One man released the air slowly; another quickly. One man had one method, involving one series of muscular actions, for closing the door and starting the car simultaneously; another had a second method,

[171]

involving another, almost antagonistic series of muscular responses. The total effect was to create interference in habit formation, a condition which brings about a lengthening of the training period and an uncertainty of response which continues to exist after the close of the training period, to the danger of the public.

There are a number of training methods which can be used in overcoming the "disturbance" element in the training program described above, but each of them, in order to bring results, must apply the knowledge of habit formation contributed by the psychologist to industry. In the development of all kinds of skill—in wrapping bundles, in working a punch press, in examining ball bearings— the training program is of utmost importance in the development of proficiency—and an important factor of the good training program is a consideration of the psychological elements involved in training for skill.

The importance of promoting the right habits has led to the construction of special devices to promote the employment of only the correct movements in their proper sequence in the development of the proper habits of operation. Many devices of this sort, and experiments involving their application, could be described. They are premised on the law established in the psychological laboratory "that the greatest efficiency results from training under such conditions that only right habits are fixed."[17]

A complete discussion of psychological contributions to training in industry would involve an analysis of whole and part methods of training as compared in experiments by Finck,[18] by Dilger,[19] and by others. It would carry

[17] POFFENBERGER, A. T., "Applied Psychology: Its Principles and Methods," 606 pp., New York, D. Appleton & Company, 1927.

[18] FINCK, E., Anlerlung in Ganzverfahren und im Teilverfahren, *Industrielle Psychotechnik*, Vol. 3, 212–216, 1926.

[19] DILGER, J., Feilübungen am Schraubstock und am Anlerngerät, *Industrielle Psychotechnik*, Vol. 6, 369–374, 1929.

us into a description of investigations leading to improved methods of work. It would lead to a consideration of the controversy between European psychologists and American efficiency engineers on the so-called best method of work, the cost of work to the worker, etc. However, such technical discussion lies outside the scope of this chapter.

There remains only to cite one or two examples of practical results that have followed from the application of

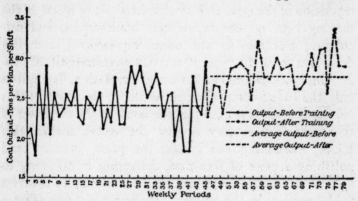

FIG. 13.—The effect of training upon the output of coal miners—weekly periods. (*After Farmer, Adams, and Stephenson.*)

psychological methods in training. Tramm,[20] for example, reports a decrease in the length of the training course and a decrease in the number of accidents following from the application of psychological principles in training motormen. The effectiveness of organized scientific training has been demonstrated by Krüger[21] in a comparison of systematically trained machinist apprentices with apprentices not profiting from systematic training. There are many other findings of the same kind, the general character of-

[20] TRAMM, K. A., Die rationelle Ausbildung des Fahrpersonals für Strassen bahnen auf psychotechnischer Grundlage, *Praktische Psychologie*, Vol. 1, Nos. 1–2, 1919.

[21] KRÜGER, G., Versuche mit verschiedenen Ausbildungs verfahren bei Maschinensclasslehrlingen, *Psychotechnische Zeitschrift*, Vol. 4, 144–158, 1929.

which is illustrated in Fig. 13 showing a comparison of output before and after training in the case of coal miners.[22]

Monotony

A problem of utmost importance in the present-day era of industrial specialization is the effect of repetitive work upon the workers' welfare and efficiency. The unceasing repetition of the same task so characteristic of work on the moving belt, on the typewriter, bookkeeping and calculating machines in the office, represents a complete departure from the type of activity characteristic of production work before the industrial revolution. It requires only the barest comparison to recognize the scope of this change. Picture, for example, the work of the carpenter of the eighteenth century sawing the wood, making his joints, assembling and gluing his parts, painting and polishing a piece of furniture, delivering it, stopping to talk with his customers and his friends, etc. In contrast is the worker in the modern furniture plant operating a saw, or sandpapering, or placing in position one item in a manufactured piece—performing the same operation, for hour after hour—frequently without any knowledge of the shape or purpose of the finished product, unable perhaps to stop for a moment of conversation for fear of holding up the progress of the work on the belt which he must tend. This constitutes so complete a change in activity, so involved and complex a problem of aptitude, that one may very well raise a question concerning the inherent suitability of mankind for such repetitive work and its effect upon the mental development and temperamental suitability of workers engaged in it.

[22] FARMER, E., S. ADAMS, and A. STEPHENSON, An Investigation in a Coal Mine, *Journal of the National Institute of Industrial Psychology*, Vol. 1, pp. 125–131, 173–181, 232–235, 1922.

The question has been raised in many diatribes and polemics on this subject. An illustration of the extreme points of view in the discussion of this subject is Marot's[23] insistence upon the evils of repetition in monotony-producing work. Marot contends that the assignment of highly specialized repetitive tasks to individual workers induces a thwarting of the creative impulse and a resulting disturbance in the adjustment of the individual worker. She contrasts with the industrial unrest of today—the strife between worker and management—the joyful cooperation of apprentices, journeymen, and master workers in the Middle Ages and Renaissance. To the participation of the latter in the entire industrial process and to the freedom which this allowed for the display of the creative impulse Marot ascribes the happiness and universal adjustment of the workers of earlier periods so well exemplified, according to her, in the pride, the social spirit, the respect for skill, of the Guilds. To the worker's lack of knowledge of his particular place in the manufacturing operation, to the boring effect of monotony, to the thwarting of the creative impulse in the ceaseless and meaningless turning of the same screw day after day, she ascribes the strife and disgruntlement which display themselves in periodic conflicts in American industry today.

Somewhat the same attitude, although oriented in the direction of the individual worker rather than from the viewpoint of industrial strife, is reflected in Mayo's[24] insistence that monotony induces pessimistic reveries, an obsessional concern on the part of the worker with his difficulties and disappointments which often ultimately result in complete maladjustment. Again, although as in

[23] MAROT, HELEN, "Creative Impulse in Industry," pp. XXII, 146, New York, E. P. Dutton & Company, 1919.

[24] MAYO, E., Basis of Industrial Psychology, *Bulletin of The Taylor Society*, Vol. 9, pp. 249–259, 1924.

the case of Marot, the explanation of the maladjustment seems perhaps oversimplified, the concern with the problem reflects the growing recognition of the mental effects of repetitive, mechanical methods of work.

It is impossible in the scope of this paper to describe in detail what may be termed the symptoms of monotony. Restlessness, yawning, loss of interest, growing difficulty in keeping at the task, an increase in the effort required to maintain efficiency are some of the many overt symptoms of monotony. Less evident on the surface, but repeatedly demonstrated in both laboratory and industrial investigations, is the inclination toward the overestimation of time intervals on the part of those engaged in monotonous work. William James has said that "a day full of excitement with no pauses is said to pass ere we know it. On the contrary, a day full of waiting, of unsatisfied desire for changes will seem a small eternity." Both English and German investigators have shown how well this applies to the numerous tasks of monotonous work.

The Monotony Curve.—Another important symptom of monotony is the characteristic nature of the progress of work during the day as reflected in the daily working curve. In work, in general, the rate of work and the amount of production tend to increase during the middle of the working spell. In other words, there is a warming up period at the beginning of the working spell, a period of relatively high production during the middle of the spell followed by a gradual and consistent drop in the rate of production. In addition, the rate of work or production tends to be fairly regular over short periods, as for example, quarter-hour periods of the working day. A rate of production distributed in this way during the day gives a daily production curve like that shown in Fig. 14, which is characteristic for many kinds of work.[25]

[25] BURTT, H. E., "Psychology and Industrial Efficiency," pp. XVIII, 395, New York, D. Appleton & Company, 1929.

Experimental studies, both in laboratory and in industry, indicate that one feature of monotony in work is the tendency for production to *fall* instead of to rise during the middle of the working spell.[26]

Boredom causes a reduced rate of working which is particularly noticeable about the middle of the spell. This decrease usually lasts from one to two hours, and during that time the average reduction in the rate of working varies from 5 to 10 per cent. It is followed by a steadier and improved rate of working as the end of the spell is approached.

Apparently, as Myers[27] has explained, the worker comes to his work feeling ready to go ahead with it, slows up in the

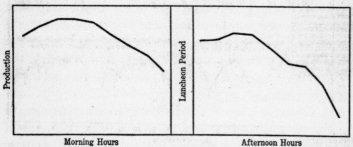

FIG. 14.—Typical daily production curve. (*After Burtt.*)

middle of the spell as he becomes bored with the work, and speeds up at the end of the day in anticipation of its end. He thus produces a curve absolutely inverse in shape to that of the normal working curve.

Variability in Production.—In addition, the production from period to period in monotonous work tends to be highly irregular.[26] "Boredom causes a more variable rate of working, which is characterized by repeated fluctuations

[26] WYATT, S., J. A. FRASER, and F. G. L. STOCK, Effects of Monotony in Work, *Industrial Fatigue Research Board, Report* 56, 47 pp., London, 1929.

[27] MYERS, C. S., "Industrial Psychology in Great Britain," 164 pp., London, Jonathan Cape, 1926.

[177]

in the time taken to complete consecutive units of output." These characteristics of production in monotonous work are well illustrated in Fig. 15. The curves representing the average rate of work during five-minute periods of a composite day are shown by the broken line whereas the general tendency is represented by the heavy black lines.

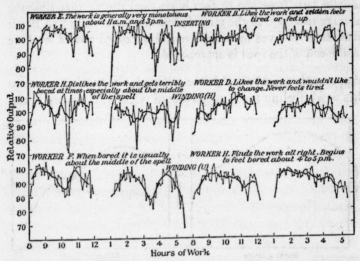

FIG. 15.—Output curves obtained when boredom was experienced (left half) and almost absent (right half) in different industrial processes. (*After Wyatt, Fraser, and Stock.*)

The workers for whom this record was made were engaged in the manufacture of electric lamps. The feeling of boredom was noted introspectively and reported. The same situation is noted in the case of a laboratory experiment on bicycle-chain assembly, where it was likewise noted

that when boredom was said to be experienced, the rate of working was particularly low about the middle of the experimental period, while the absence of boredom was conducive to a higher and uniform rate of working throughout the spell. In the former case, however, an appreciable improvement in the rate of working occurred in the penultimate stage of work.

Other symptoms of monotony may be noted, but those which have been discussed are sufficient to indicate the importance of monotony and perhaps to explain the psychologist's concern with the possible harmful effects of the highly specialized industrial task.

Difference in Individual Susceptibility to Monotony.—This concern may perhaps be looked upon as one of only academic interest by the industrial leader who insists that the highly repetitive process is necessary to maintain the demands of quantity production and who is convinced that the efficiency of the individual worker is directly proportionate to the degree of automatization of his work. The industrial leader may even feel that any procedure which substitutes variety in work for uniformity can do nothing but interfere with the productive efficiency of his plant. He questions the incidence of pessimistic daydreaming and its attendant ills and the insistence upon the generally harmful effects of so-called monotonous work. He is perhaps inclined to accept too readily the questionable discovery of Goddard, so widely held by the intelligentsia who read the *American Mercury*, that the average American is a moron and does not deserve a better fate anyhow. He may even frankly state that his responsibility to the worker is a limited one, and that the worker can seek employment elsewhere in more varied work if he fails to find happiness or becomes irritated or overfatigued in the specialized job in which he is engaged.

Whatever may be the position of management, it is safe to assume that it will be interested in reliable *evidence* on the susceptibility of the worker to the harmful effects of a repetitive job, on the exact effect of uniformity and variety in work on production, and on similar questions which

[179]

must be raised in any scientific study of the nature and influence of monotony in industry.

Susceptibility to monotony in work has been the subject of a number of investigations conducted both in the laboratory and in the industrial plant. Foremost among the problems to be investigated is that of whether all individuals are equally susceptible to the harmful effects of monotonous work. Among employment managers and among industrial executives in general, there is, for example, more than a suspicion that there exists a direct relationship between general intelligence and monotony. One executive has gone as far as to say that the real problem of modern industry is to find a large enough number of feeble-minded adults to fill the repetitive jobs to which individuals of high intelligence cannot adjust themselves.

The belief that low susceptibility to the feeling of boredom on repetitive work is associated with low intelligence, has been justified in a number of investigations. So, for example, in a study of department-store wrappers and cashiers, the writer[28] found a distinctly higher turnover among girls with higher intelligence test scores than among those with median scores. Kornhauser[29] reports similar findings in a survey of office occupations. Burnett,[30] an English investigator, employed four girls for a period of two months on daily repetitive work of cross-stitching. Of the four girls A and B were very intelligent; C was of average intelligence and D was of low intelligence. The production of these girls is shown in Fig. 16. The two most intelligent girls, A and B, although capable of reaching a high output from time to time, proved unable to maintain

[28] Viteles, M. S., Selecting Cashiers and Predicting Length of Service, *The Journal of Personnel Research*, Vol. 2, pp. 467–473, 1924.

[29] Kornhauser, A. W., Some Business Applications of a Mental Alertness Test, *The Journal of Personnel Research*, Vol. 1, pp. 103–121, 1922.

[30] Burnett, I., An Experimental Investigation of Repetitive Work, *Journal of the National Institute of Industrial Psychology*, Vol. 2, pp. 18–23, 1924.

it and showed unmistakable signs of boredom in restlessness, yawning, frequent change of posture, etc. It is of

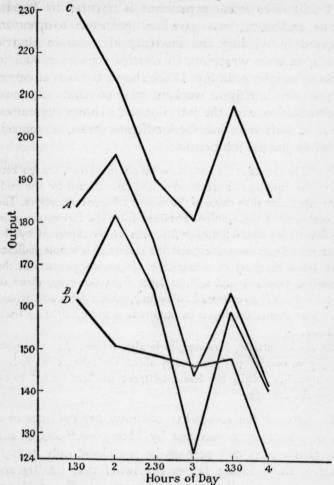

FIG. 16.—Average periodic output of four subjects for Tuesday afternoon of sixth, seventh, and eighth weeks. No rest pause. Curves *a*, *b*, and *c* are examples of the "monotony curve." (*After Burnett.*)

interest to note that the curves of the more intelligent workers show the drop in the middle spell of work which

[181]

has claimed to be so closely associated with the feeling of boredom in work.

A still more recent experiment is reported by Wyatt, Fraser, and Stock,[31] who gave intelligence tests to operators engaged in winding and inserting filaments in electric lamps, in soap wrapping, in chocolate packing, and in tobacco weighing. In Fig. 17 are shown the output curves of the more intelligent workers, most of whom expressed dissatisfaction with the job. Figure 18 shows the output curve of girls with inferior intelligence who, in general, failed to find the job tiresome.

It will be seen that the output curves obtained from the workers of inferior intelligence are steadier and less affected by the mid-spell depression than those of the more intelligent operatives. The general tone of the opinions obtained from the former group of workers is also very different from the views expressed by the more intelligent operatives; and the results as a whole indicate that, while the workers of inferior intelligence appear to like the repetitive processes and seldom suffer from boredom, those of superior intelligence seemed to be industrial misfits and would have been better employed in occupations more suited to their abilities.

At the same time, however, it is also evident that the more intelligent operatives were usually above the average in productive efficiency, while the less intelligent workers tended to be below the average.

In spite of the somewhat contradictory evidence in a recent laboratory experiment by Thompson,[32] and of the fact that results may perhaps be considered only as suggestive, the evidence favors the belief that intelligence plays some part in the creation of monotony. This evidence represents a distinct contribution on the part of the psy-

[31] WYATT, S., J. A. FRASER, and F. G. L. STOCK, Effects of Monotony in Work, *Industrial Fatigue Research Board, Report* 56, 47 pp., London, 1929.

[32] THOMPSON, L. A., JR., Measuring Susceptibility to Monotony, *The Personnel Journal*, Vol. 8, pp. 172–196, 1929.

chologist toward individual adjustment in industry and in promoting industrial efficiency.

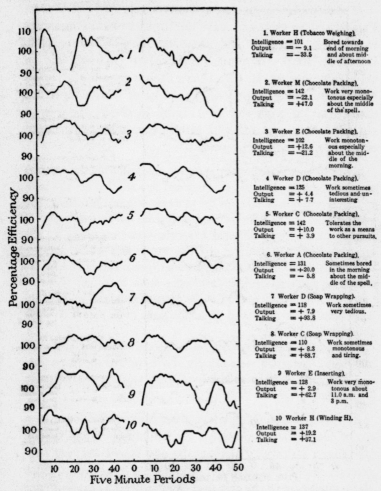

1. Worker H (Tobacco Weighing).

Intelligence = 101	Bored towards
Output = − 9.1	end of morning
Talking = −33.5	and about mid-dle of afternoon

2. Worker M (Chocolate Packing).

Intelligence = 142	Work very mono-tonous especially
Output = −22.1	about the middle
Talking = +47.0	of the spell.

3. Worker E (Chocolate Packing).

Intelligence = 102	Work monoton-ous especially
Output = +12.6	about the mid-dle of the
Talking = −21.2	morning.

4. Worker D (Chocolate Packing).

Intelligence = 125	Work sometimes
Output = + 4.4	tedious and un-interesting
Talking = + 7.7	

5. Worker C (Chocolate Packing).

Intelligence = 142	Tolerates the
Output = +10.0	work as a means
Talking = + 3.9	to other pursuits.

6. Worker A (Chocolate Packing).

Intelligence = 131	Sometimes bored
Output = +20.0	in the morning
Talking = − 5.8	about the mid-dle of the spell.

7 Worker D (Soap Wrapping).

Intelligence = 118	Work sometimes
Output = + 7.9	very tedious.
Talking = +93.8	

8. Worker C (Soap Wrapping).

Intelligence = 110	Work sometimes
Output = + 8.3	monotonous
Talking = +88.7	and tiring.

9 Worker E (Inserting).

Intelligence = 128	Work very mono-tonous about
Output = + 2.9	11.0 a.m. and
Talking = +62.7	3 p.m.

10 Worker H (Winding H).

Intelligence = 137	
Output = +19.2	
Talking = +37.1	

FIG. 17.—Output curves obtained from workers of superior intelligence. (*After Wyatt, Fraser, and Stock.*)

The existence of differences in temperamental make-up remains to be investigated. That temperamental factors do

[183]

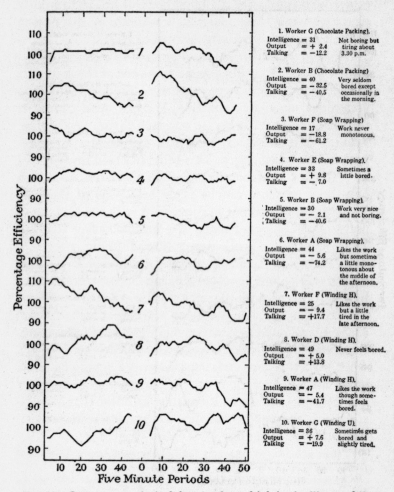

1. Worker G (Chocolate Packing).
Intelligence = 31   Not boring but
Output   = + 2.4   tiring about
Talking   = −12.2   3.30 p.m.

2. Worker B (Chocolate Packing)
Intelligence = 40   Very seldom
Output   = −32.5   bored except
Talking   = −40.5   occasionally in
                      the morning.

3. Worker F (Soap Wrapping)
Intelligence = 17   Work never
Output   = −18.8   monotonous.
Talking   = −61.2

4. Worker E (Soap Wrapping).
Intelligence = 33   Sometimes a
Output   = + 9.8   little bored.
Talking   = − 7.0

5. Worker B (Soap Wrapping).
Intelligence = 30   Work very nice
Output   = − 2.1   and not boring.
Talking   = −40.6

6. Worker A (Soap Wrapping).
Intelligence = 44   Likes the work
Output   = −5.6   but sometime
Talking   = −74.2   a little mono-
                      tonous about
                      the middle of
                      the afternoon.

7. Worker F (Winding H).
Intelligence = 25   Likes the work
Output   = − 9.4   but a little
Talking   = +17.7   tired in the
                      late afternoon.

8. Worker D (Winding H).
Intelligence = 49   Never feels bored.
Output   = + 5.0
Talking   = +13.8

9. Worker A (Winding H).
Intelligence = 47   Likes the work
Output   = − 5.4   though some-
Talking   = −41.7   times feels
                      bored.

10. Worker G (Winding U).
Intelligence = 36   Sometimes gets
Output   = + 7.6   bored and
Talking   = −19.9   slightly tired.

Percentage Efficiency

Five Minute Periods

Fig. 18.—Output curves obtained from workers of inferior intelligence. (*After Wyatt, Fraser, and Stock.*)

play an important part is suggested in the laboratory studies by Thompson,[33] Wunderlich,[34] Winkler,[35] and others who emphasize the importance of fitting to highly repetitive work those individuals who are by disposition and temperament especially adapted to it.

The Effect of Uniformity and Variety in Work upon Monotony.—Uniformity in work seems to be one of the constants in the monotony-producing situation. The insistence upon uniformity, upon specialization, is based upon the belief that keeping the worker at one task favors production, whereas variation of any kind from task to task interferes with industrial efficiency. This belief has been investigated in a number of laboratory and plant studies, to which only brief reference can be made here. One of these by Wyatt[36] was carried out in connection with the packing of drugs in the shipping room of a manufacturing concern. Three schedules of work were followed. In one, the drugs were assembled, counted, packed, and wrapped by each worker; the second involved a change in occupation every half hour; in the third the same work was done throughout the day. The schedule involving *many* (that is, half-hour) changes was found to be least efficient. On the other hand, there was found little difference in efficiency between the work involving few variations and work involving strict uniformity. Observations on the part of the investigator and introspective reports led to the conclusion that "repetitive work throughout the day was conducive to fatigue, boredom, and monotony."

[33] THOMPSON, L. A., JR., Measuring Susceptibility to Monotony, *The Personnel Journal*, Vol. 8, pp. 172–196, 1929.

[34] WUNDERLICH, H., Die Einwirking einförmiger zwangsläufiger Arbeit auf die Persönlichkeitstruktur, *Zeitschrift zur psychologische Berufswissens*, Vol. 31, 53 pp., 1925.

[35] WINKLER, A., Die Monotonie der Arbeit, *Zeitschrift zur psychologische Berufswissens*, Vol. 19, 45 pp., 1922.

[36] WYATT, S., The Effect of Changes in Activity, *Industrial Fatigue Research Board*, *Report* 26, London, 1924.

In a more recent study Wyatt and Fraser[37] analyze the effect of variety as compared with uniformity of work in soap wrapping, in handkerchief folding, in bicycle-chain assembling, in cigarette making, and in cartridge-case assembling. So, for example, in handkerchief folding, repeated folding into the same design was alternated with

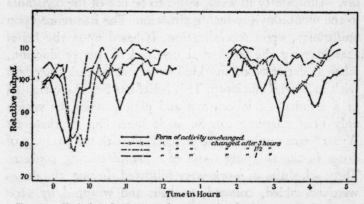

FIG. 19.—Variations in the rate of work produced when the form of activity is changed at different times within the spell of work (cigarette making). (*After Wyatt and Fraser.*)

folding into another shape. In cigarette making, the rolling of cigarettes over the entire day was alternated with cutting and with variations of cutting and making. Typical results are shown in Fig. 19.

Each curve indicates the output produced in consecutive five minute periods throughout the day, expressed as a percentage of the average output on days of continuous unvaried activity. The depressions in the curves observed in the early part of the morning spell were due to interruptions caused by one or more of the operatives taking lunch, which occurred at slightly different times on different days.

[37] WYATT, S. and J. A. FRASER, The Comparative Effects of Variety and Uniformity in Work: A Preliminary Inquiry, *Industrial Fatigue Research Board, Report* 52, 36 pp., London, 1928.

When the workers knew that the form of work would be changed after three hours of uniform activity, a somewhat different type of output curve was obtained. In the first place, the output following the luncheon interval was higher and free from the depression observed on the days of uniform activity, a feature of some interest, since it might be expected that the first three hours of work would yield approximately similar curves in both cases. The afternoon curve is similar in tendency to the one previously described, but is on a higher level and has a more pronounced final spurt.

When the change occurred at the end of the 1½ hours, the *beneficial* effects were still more marked. The output in the latter half of the morning spell was the highest recorded in any of the experimental series, and was also high in the initial and final stages of the afternoon spell. Although in the latter spell there was a reduction in output in the intervening period, the extent of the decrease was very much less than in the two previous cases. Somewhat similar tendencies were noticeable when the same form of activity was never continued for more than an hour, and the output curve approached more closely to a horizontal straight line.

The operatives were unanimous in the opinion that the cutting operation, when continued for long periods was very tiring. As a result, accuracy of movement was impaired and the ends of the cigarette paper were sometimes cut away together with the surplus tobacco. Making cigarettes, on the other hand, was said to be comparatively pleasant and was more conducive to boredom than to fatigue.

At the same time, the opinions of the operatives suggested that the varied activities were more satisfying than the results indicate, since they were unanimous and emphatic in their preference for the varied method.

The results of this investigation favor the view that complete uniformity in manual repetitive work is generally less productive and leads to greater irregularity in the rate of working than a reasonable degree of variety, which is also preferred by the workers, though this effect seems to depend partly on the nature of the process and partly on the individual operative. Furthermore, while frequent changes are definitely detrimental to production, there is some evidence that the best conditions are attained when the form of activity is changed after $1\frac{1}{2}$ to 2 hours of unvaried work.

Again, as in the case of susceptibility to monotony, considerable work remains to be done, but the evidence that variation in activity can be introduced into industry without interfering with production is in itself important. Its greatest significance follows from the fact that variation is in most instances followed by increased satisfaction on the part of the worker. A fertile avenue of increased individual adjustment in industry at no economic loss is opened by this finding.

Other experimental approaches and findings could be cited. Significant from the viewpoint of practical improvements is the finding that time-piece systems of payment seem less conducive to the feeling to boredom than the day-rate systems. The possibility of greater earnings, the competitive feature, seems to induce interest, to set up a goal which counterbalances the effect of boredom or perhaps compensates for the "set" or attitude toward monotony on the part of the worker. Rest pauses properly spaced do much toward changing the shape of the production curve in a repetitive job and toward decreasing the expressed discontent. Short pauses for conversation and the development of group morale are other agencies for putting into its proper place this industrial pest—boredom at work.

Problems of Individual Adjustment

At the risk of repetition, it seems well to revert to a point of view touched upon in an earlier portion of this chapter. This concerns the psychologist's viewpoint with respect to the individual worker. The individual at work is the ultimate factor with which the industrial psychologist is concerned. The latter seeks to make industry more efficient, but he believes that in the final analysis this can only be accomplished by considering the maximum welfare of each worker in industry. In formulating the program of industrial psychology, the maximum efficiency of the individual and his greatest happiness are looked upon as complementary facets of a single objective.

This orientation of industrial psychology has led, in recent years, to a shift in emphasis from adjustment through selection alone to the study of maladjustments on the part of employed workers and to their correction. There is a growing recognition that efficiency in production and the happiness of the individual worker are dependent not alone upon selection, as completely organized along scientific lines as that may be, but at least equally as much upon the readjustment of the employed worker. Such readjustment involves the application of what has been described as the *clinical method* in industry. The *clinical method in psychology* is nothing more than a weighting of every factor which may effect the adjustment of the individual worker in terms of his adjustment. It refers to the consideration and weighting of aptitude, temperamental traits, interest, working conditions, and other factors which may lead to maladjustment of an employed worker in an attempt to promote to his better adaptation in the industrial organization of which he is a member.

To even the most optimistic industrial psychologist, the possibilities of improved selection seem limited by the inherent weakness of test procedures and by variations in the behavior of mankind other than those of ability and temperament. He knows that the variables in the capacity to carry on a job are often too many or too complex to make perfect prediction possible. He knows further that the adjustment of the employee is determined by many other factors than ability to perform the job and that, even if the selection instruments were perfect, maladjustment

[189]

would still take place and labor turnover would still appear on the monthly report of the employment manager.

This reflects no discouragement with psychological tests and other improved methods of selection in industry. It is merely a frank recognition of their limitations. The selective procedure is extremely useful in eliminating from employment a large proportion of those who are clearly unsuited to the work. It is probably the best single and the most economical method for decreasing the incidence of maladjustment among employees. But, regardless of the value of the tests, maladjustments will still appear among employees subsequent to employment. In addition, in every organization there is a large group of employees hired prior to the installation of scientific selection procedures who exhibit incompetency in their work, dissatisfaction on the job. Such maladjustment can be considerably reduced through the application of proper methods.

The application of this point of view may be illustrated from a study made by the writer[38] in the taxicab business. In the organization in which the study was made, as in the case of almost every other similar organization, wages are paid in the form of commission on earnings. In the present instance, drivers received $33\frac{1}{3}$ per cent of their collections, supplemented, of course, by tips, which provide a considerable addition to earnings.

The analysis of the earnings of drivers hired during 1924 and still in the employ of the company at the time of the study, showed an average difference in earnings of over $600 per year between the 25 per cent best earners and the 25 per cent poorest earners. There was a maximum difference of over $1,000 a year. A study of the mental, physical, social, and economic factors affecting earnings showed that

[38] VITELES, M. S., The Clinical Method in Industry, *Industrial Psychology*, Vol. 1, pp. 753-758, 1926.

such factors as age, marital conditions, number of jobs during the years prior to employment by this company, and physical condition affected adjustment, and that data on these factors could be used in the elimination of a proportion of poor earners prior to employment.

But, and this is possibly the most important contribution of the study, there was shown to be significant differences in the causation of maladjustment *in individual cases*. Poor health made it impossible for one man to work as steadily as required for good earnings. In the case of another, inadequate incentives held a more prominent position. Still others showed temperamental unsuitability for the job. The multiplicity of causes in the case of all the poor earners, and the dominance of a single cause in the case of each individual earner suggested the possibility of attempting to readjust poor earners on the basis of a careful study of each individual case.

This analysis of the causes of the failure on the part of the individual was made jointly by a group consisting of a garage superintendent, the street supervisor, the medical director, the social worker, and the psychologist. The psychologist tabulated, organized, and interpreted data obtained from all of these individuals, from the very complete personnel records maintained in the organization, and from a clinical interview with the cab driver.

The findings were presented in terms of definite recommendations at the meeting of the group described above. There is not the space to cite typical case studies, but the application of this method made possible the readjustment of approximately 50 per cent of men who without an analysis of the situation would have been discharged as the easiest way of handling their ineffectiveness in the organization.

Similar clinics have been established by a number of transportation companies, including companies in Cleveland,[39] Milwaukee,[40] Boston,[41] etc. for the readjustment of employees frequently involved in accidents.

Just as a physician diagnoses and treats a chronic ailment to effect a cure, so those employees who are repeatedly involved in accidents or are *accident-prone* are being studied and treated individually in the belief that many of them may be adjusted properly and become assets rather than liabilities. Case study methods, while reducing accident frequency among the small group of high-accident men, tend at the same time to encourage the entire group of employees to improve their records by breaking down the age-worn theory that accidents are a matter of "hard luck" and that they can not be prevented.[39]

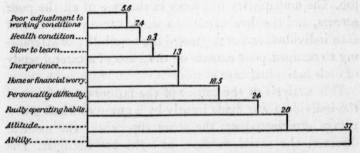

FIG. 20.—Causative factors in accident proneness. (*After Shellow.*)

A recent report on the work of the Milwaukee clinic shows the distribution of major items in accident proneness to be that indicated in Fig. 20.

The character of the final analysis made in individual cases and the type of recommendations arrived at as a result of these clinical studies can be illustrated by citations

[39] The Accident Prone Employe, A Study of Electric Railway Operation undertaken by The Cleveland Railway Company, with the co-operation of Policyholders Service Bureau, Metropolitan Life Insurance Company, 26 pp., 1930.

[40] SHELLOW, S. M., The Accident Clinic, How It Functions and What it Accomplishes, *The Journal of Personnel Research*, Vol. 9, pp. 203–215, 1930.

[41] BINGHAM, W. V., Personality and Public Accidents; a Study of Accident Prone Drivers, *Reprint and Circular Series of the Personnel Research Federation*, No. 18, 1928.

from one or two case studies, reported by the Cleveland Company.[42]

MOTORMAN A

Observation of Operation: (Two Observations).—The subject demonstrates average skill in handling his car, as might reasonably be expected from his vehicle collision record. On the whole, he watches traffic closely, distributing his attention well and observing ordinary precautions in following traffic and in checking his car when uncertainty arises. He is particularly alert for vehicles approaching from the rear to anticipate a possible "cut-in."

Apparently, the outstanding causative factor of accidents, as shown by observation, is his inability or failure to judge speed and distance accurately. He repeatedly checks the car quickly when approaching a vehicle, even though often there is ample time to make a smooth stop, or when he should have proceeded without checking the car at all. His sudden stops under these conditions are rough and jerky, which clearly account for his exceptionally high record of "falls in car," as well as for those collisions caused by vehicles striking the rear of the car. When making a regular stop or start, his operation is generally smooth.

Personal Interview.—A is a steady, plodding, conscientious type of man who is trying to do his work well. His intelligence is average and his domestic life happy for the most part. His health is good and he appears contented with his work. The subject is farsighted and has been compelled to wear double vision glasses at work for eight years. When told of his difficulty in judging distance accurately as shown by his tendency to make unnecessarily fast stops, he was unwilling to grant that his eyes were the cause. He became argumentative and, moreover, he demanded an explanation of what constituted an unnecessarily fast stop. He finally agreed, however, to have his eyes examined by a competent oculist and have his glasses changed, if advisable. He had little comment to make regarding his accidents, giving the impression that too much weight was being attached to them.

[42] *Op. cit.*

Treatment:

1. That his eyes be examined by a competent oculist, and that he be followed up to see that he secures proper corrective glasses if his present pair is found inadequate.

2. Following this, that his operation be checked closely and reinstruction be given if necessary.

MOTORMAN B

Observation of Operation: (Three Observations).—Under normal conditions the subject handles his car satisfactorily from an operating standpoint, making good starts and stops and paying strict attention to business. In traffic he exercises good judgment, gauges distance accurately and appears to be skillful in keeping his car under control in tight places.

However, when he becomes late his operation undergoes a radical change. He becomes sullen, keeping his eyes fixed upon the track immediately before him rather than remaining alert to conditions at both his right and left. When spoken to by inspectors, he assumes a hostile attitude. At such times he also displays an impatience and hostility toward passengers. When in this frame of mind, apparently, he becomes indifferent to his responsibilities. Outstanding perhaps is his failure to pay attention to vehicles passing him, particularly those approaching from the rear. He also makes very rough starts and stops, exerting little effort to get his car under control until a collision impends.

This sullen and indifferent state of mind is clearly the principal causative factor of accidents in which he is involved. Secondly, there is the factor of unwillingness to shoulder the full responsibilities of the job, as confirmed by the fact that his record shows 29 per cent of all collisions happened within the first hour of duty, which in 65 per cent of the cases was from 5:30 A. M. to 6:30 A. M. when traffic is extremely light.

Personal Interview: (Two Occasions).—The subject's attitude was one of marked indifference during the entire interview. He became bored, looked at his watch and appeared to be anxious to get away, although there was no cause for being in a hurry, he later stated. He seemed unconcerned about his accident record; none of the accidents were his fault, just a matter of "hard luck."

[194]

Later he became somewhat argumentative and complained of his run and heavy loads, "not getting a square deal; picked on by inspectors, etc." At no time was he willing to grant that he might be at fault occasionally. The subject was married, but is now divorced and is living alone. He has had two years of high school education, talks readily and appears well above the average intelligence. He owns a car, deriving most of his pleasure in life from that, apparently.

His health is good, he stated, although later he complained of catarrh, sore back and weak eyes.

He stated that he liked his work, as otherwise he would not stay. At the close of the interview, when asked what he was going to do to better his record, he offered no hope of being able to make any improvement.

Treatment:

1. That inspectors and those of his superiors with whom his personality clashes be informed of his mental characteristics and be asked to make a special effort to approach him with a friendly attitude.

2. That failing to show an improvement within the month, his case be referred to the Superintendent of Transportation for review and disciplinary action.

The character of the results obtained from such clinical studies of older employees are illustrated in Fig. 21 showing the frequency rates for each of forty-four accident-prone motormen in Cleveland and embodying a comparison of accidents before and after the study of each man.

The combined rate of the forty-four motormen was 1.31 accidents per thousand miles in 1928, while during 1929 it dropped to 0.75, equivalent to a reduction of 42.7 per cent. All but three individuals showed a reduction in rating, and in two of these cases treatment was postponed indefinitely because of company policy.

Similar results are reported by The Milwaukee Electric Railway and Light Company.[43] The reduction over the

[43] Shellow, S. M., The Accident-Clinic, How It Functions and What It Accomplishes, *The Journal of Personnel Research*, Vol. 9, pp. 203–215, 1930.

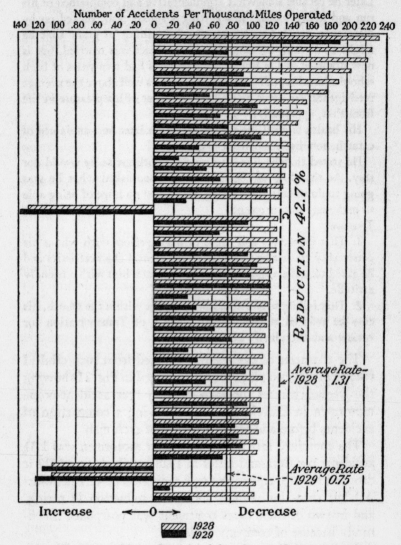

FIG. 21.—Frequency rates for each of forty-four accident-prone motormen showing comparison before and following study, 1928 and 1929, Woodhill Division, The Cleveland Railway Company.

system as a whole, including the group studied in the accident clinic, was 25 per cent from January 1, 1929, to January 1, 1930. Over the same period, a reduction in accidents of the special group studied in the accident clinic was 81.5 per cent, and in addition, the average accident per man was reduced from 2.8 to 0.51, which is below the average from the entire group of men.

In Boston similarly satisfactory results have been obtained through the clinical study of transportation employees in accordance with a program developed under the direction of Dr. W. V. Bingham[44] of the Personnel Research Federation.

In reporting these results, it is important to bear in mind that the improvement as a result of clinical study was shown not in earnings and accident rate alone, but in the attitude of the men toward the job and in the satisfaction derived from the job. All who have conducted clinics of this kind point to these as important sequelae of the employment of the clinical method in industry.

Other examples of the application of the clinical method can be cited. They are found in the work of one or two psychiatrists who have concerned themselves with case studies in industry. They find perhaps a sounder exemplification in the work of the clinical psychologist, who as a scientific observer trained in the interpretation of objective facts, with his common-sense orientation of the normal, free from a predominant concern with the abnormalities of human conduct, the Freudian obsessions, the reveries, etc., so characteristic of the psychiatrist, is perhaps best qualified to promote the type of individual adjustment in industry which is fundamental to the efficient functioning of the industrial enterprise.

[44] BINGHAM, W. V., Personality and Public Accidents; a Study of Accident Prone Drivers, *Reprint and Circular Series of the Personnel Research Federation*, No. 18, 1928.

It has been necessary to omit from this chapter reference to other important applications of psychology in industry. Investigations on fatigue, on the effects of noise, on the influence of distraction, etc., have led to additional contributions which cannot be discussed here. If the author has given a brief indication of the significance of psychology in promoting individual welfare in industry, and of its concrete accomplishments, this chapter will have served its purpose.

Chapter VII

PSYCHOLOGY IN RELATION TO SOCIAL AND POLITICAL PROBLEMS

by FLOYD H. ALLPORT

WITH THE COOPERATION OF MILTON C. DICKENS AND RICHARD L. SCHANCK

I

IN the task of bringing psychology to bear upon contemporary problems, we are faced at the outset by the necessity of revising our definitions. Our conceptions, both of psychology and of the social sciences, must be altered. Laws of behavior and introspective reports of consciousness as revealed in the psychological laboratory, however interesting and important for the study of the solitary individual, have not been of much help in predicting the behavior of individuals in the free relationships of daily social life. While we should not forget that psychology is, after all, a science of individual organisms, still we must see these individuals in somewhat broader contexts than those in which we observe them in the laboratory. Our science may lose exactness through this procedure; nevertheless it seems to be the only way in which the psychologist can be of service in the complex problems with which our social and political leaders are now struggling.

Of no less significance is the change in viewpoint which will be necessary regarding social science. We must have a new definition of social organization, social institutions, and society; for we can no longer operate under the fiction of a super-individual order operated for human ends through industry and machinery, an order to which the individual is somehow to be adjusted. Industrial and educational psychologists, as well as personnel workers, have long cherished such a point of view. They have conceived their job as the task of using psychological principles in helping to adjust individuals to the social system. The work of the social psychologist, as I conceive it, is a direct challenge to such a program. My present purpose is to place the old social problems in a new light, and to get, if possible, a more complete view of the picture. I conceive my task as a social psychologist to be the study of the behavior of individuals in association with other individuals; and my purpose is not the adjustment of the individual to society, but the study of the social system itself as a part of individuals. Instead of thinking of the social order as something which includes and is composed of individuals, we shall take the opposite viewpoint, namely, that individuals contain within their habits of behavior that system which we call the social order.

In such an approach the main interest is focused upon a twofold manner of viewing the facts of human behavior. We have, on the one hand, behavior as a collection of uniform and reciprocal responses of a vast number of individuals, that is, behavior from a "common-segment" or "institutional" point of view. This is the field of primary interest to the social scientist. The other view is that of the individual psychologist, or the psychological clinician, who sees not the common behavior segment of many individuals, but all the segments of the behavior of a single individual. This latter is the viewpoint of the whole personality. A human being is the meeting ground of these two points of view; and the major social problems, in my opinion, are due to the conflict of these approaches within the individual himself and to the maladjustments produced by the necessity, in our modern complex society, of bringing them together. Human beings are not machines, though our social arrangements often compel them to act as though they were.

A word of caution is needed at this point. We do not mean that an individual contains within himself these two aspects as sharply divided fields of living. His personality in all its uniqueness is not clearly separated from the things which he does as a member of groups and organizations. Frequently an individual expresses himself through the organizations to which he belongs. Our aim in this analysis is logically to separate, for the purpose of understanding, the things which relate to the expression of unique traits, and the things which relate to the *common* behavior of the group through which the individual achieves expression. For example, the kinds of organizations the subject will choose to belong to, provided it is possible for him to make a choice, may exhibit traits characteristic of his personality. Or again, if he is an executive in a business or an educational institution, there may be considerable flexibility in his role in that organization, so that his unique characteristics may emerge in the manner in which he discharges his office. But ultimately there will be limits of spontaneity: certain kinds of things must be done in certain ways by all who are playing a given societal role. And as we go downward toward the rank and file (for example, to the manual workers in a factory), we find a greater degree of stereotyped common behavior and a smaller range of the things in which the individual can exhibit characteristics of behavior peculiar wholly to himself. Life everywhere is an interpenetration of these two aspects of behavior. Their clear separation comes not in the organism as an object of study but in our purpose or point of view toward life. Nevertheless, for the study of social problems this distinction of viewpoint is very important; for regardless of whether these classes of behavior are separated in the

[201]

individuals behaving or not, they are clearly distinguished in the attitude of the individualist toward the conduct of human affairs as compared with that of the institutionalist. We have, in other words, two practical philosophies at work, the one making whole individuals in all their uniqueness the center of the picture, and the other focusing effort upon a reciprocal working of activities which are only segments of individuals. The extent to which the conflict of these two viewpoints is involved in our major social problems is insufficiently realized.

One way of characterizing the contrast we have been discussing is by speaking of the institutionalist viewpoint as one of *partial inclusion*. This means that regardless of the number of organizations or relationships a person participates in, what he does in those relationships is by the nature of the case limited to a certain kind of behavior. It is not possible for *any* kind of response to follow the stimulus presented in the given situation. For example, upon entering the subway, we drop our fare in the box. Many individuals are here exhibiting substantially the same segment of behavior. It is true that there will be minor individual variations in the manner in which this is done. One individual may do it with a slightly different gesture from another; one may "pinch the nickel" a little harder than another. A third may look about to see if there is some means of getting through without dropping the nickel. But the range of things which can be done is at best very restricted in this situation. There is little hope, for example, of using our various personality traits and gifts of persuasion upon the keeper of the subway gate. All too often there is no keeper at all, but only a machine which automatically releases the gate when a five-cent piece is deposited in the slot. One characteristic of common-segment behavior is that it can usually be elicited and controlled by machines substituted for persons quite as readily as by persons themselves. It is only in those situations where the unexpected act has an opportunity to occur, that is to say, where the entire range of the personality, potentially, can be expressed, that the machine system breaks down.

I suppose no one has ever counted them, but the number of such situations with which we are faced in modern urban life, occasions, that is, in which a certain uniformity and restriction of behavior is demanded, must be very great. Among tradespeople, salesmen, factory and clerical workers, the number of these occasions is probably greater than in many other vocations. This stereotyping of behavior, obviously cannot absorb all of our reactions, even in the most congested and highly mechanized urban areas. There remain some occasions upon which we behave according to a "law of our own nature" rather than according to the law of the institution in which we function. It is apparently a matter of degree; and in this conflict between the partial inclusion demanded by institutional or cultural behavior and the total inclusion natural to the original biological nature of mankind as a part of the animal kingdom there lies the root of many a dilemma of modern life.

In a sense it is somewhat mystical to talk about an "individual" or a "personality" just as it is mystical to talk about the "controlling power of an institution." But we do not have to settle the question of what personalities and institutions are in themselves. All we need to think about is concrete instances of conduct and what we want to do about them. Whether we stress the individual personality or the social institutions will depend upon the kind of behavior we are looking for and are desirous of predicting; and vice versa. The more we organize life into economic, political, religious, or other institutions, the greater the number of instances of uniform, common-

[203]

segment, behavior we shall obtain. These instances will reflect the general pattern of culture, but will not enable us to differentiate between individuals. We can predict further restricted behavior of every individual from the behavior already observed; but we cannot predict the unrestricted behavior which we may expect from any one individual. If all of life were like the dropping of the nickel in the fare box, we should have a remarkable facility in predicting human behavior; but the behavior we should predict would be of a very special type—that, namely, in which every one conformed, and in which, therefore, we could detect no trace of that which we call an individual. We should predict what a person would do in a given situation precisely because we should expect him to behave like every other individual in our past observation of that type of situation. If, on the other hand, we should eliminate fare boxes and all similar contrivances from our civilization, we should have little or no ability in predicting common-segment behavior, for there would be little opportunity either for forming universal habits or for observing them in operation; but we might be able to predict behavior of another sort, namely, the behavior which individual A would exhibit precisely because he is individual A and not individual B. That is, we might observe A reacting without any outside controls upon his behavior in so many different kinds of situations that we might be able to tell what he would do in the next and somewhat novel situation. We might, in other words, discover certain traits which are characteristic of individual A and not characteristic of any particular social situation. This, it will be readily seen, is a type of result we could never accomplish from our observation of people performing common, institutional habits. But it will be prediction of something altogether different.

Prediction is a step toward the objective of control. When we know what sort of behavior will follow from a certain kind of social regulation or its absence, we are in a position to cultivate that type of behavior or to allow it to be unexpressed as we desire. When we have both these possibilities (the individualistic and the institutional) before us we are free to choose with an understanding of what we are doing. We are free to set the stage, as it were, for the production either of behavior characteristic of separate individuals, or behavior common to a large number of human beings classed under some group or organization. We can foster either that which we regard as the best opportunity for individual self-expression, or that which we consider to be the best form of society.

It has been the contention of many social scientists that these two aims mean one and the same thing. Minimizing the distinction we have made between the two ways of viewing and classifying behavior, some sociologists have asserted that the most perfect form of society is that in which there is the fullest degree of individual self-expression and opportunity. This assertion, however, seems to me merely a pious wish impossible of fulfillment, unless we mean by "society" merely a collection of altruistic individuals. As soon as society as an ordering, or an organization, of social behavior appears, the emergence of common-segment alignments, with their encroachment upon the total inclusion of personalities, seems inescapable. Let us test the truth of this statement by a few examples.

II

We shall consider first the problem of consolidation in merchandising which has resulted in such phenomena as the chain store and the chain gasoline filling station. Those who look at commercial behavior from the standpoint of the common-segment, or the economic institution, have as their goal a high degree of standardization and adjustment of actions of individuals, so that commercial transactions can be achieved with the minimum of cost and labor and with a maximum, therefore, of profits. In part this end is gained by the development of machinery of production and transportation, and in part by economies in organization. Looking at the segment of mercantile behavior alone, it has been found that the handling of great quantities of merchandise under a central head is more economical than the conduct of business in a small way by the small local entrepreneur. In the great centers of population, where life has become so divided into segments of reciprocal division of labor that a few more compartments would make little difference, the chain-store idea has taken root and has spread rapidly. In other sections, on the other hand, where people are still accustomed to intimate, face-to-face community life, a bitter opposition against this system has revealed itself. In communities, for example, where life is organized around whole personalities, the merchant is not merely a man who hands goods over a counter and takes money in return; he is an acquaintance of his customers in many other relationships, and sometimes a close friend. In such a community, moreover, the customers know that the money which the merchant receives he will spend for the most part locally, with the result of a fostering of economic prosperity in all directions within that local region. Clearly, in this earlier scheme there was a chance for the inclusion of a far greater degree of personality in economic transactions than in the great cities with their chain merchandizing systems. For this reason consolidated retail methods with distant control have met with bitter opposition by those who value the local and personal phases of business; and yet, because of their great advantage for the economic segment alone (that is, goods can be handled more cheaply, with lower prices to the customer and greater profits to the few in control) such methods are becoming widely intrenched and are altering our civiliza-

[206]

tion in a profound way. We have traveled in the direction of a more economically efficient social order, but at the expense of taking away many of the earlier opportunities of individuals for entering with their whole personalities and their full interests into the economic life of the community. A variety of goods and new inventions are obtained more cheaply by the consumer—and this represents the more highly perfected societal organization; but the full expression of all the consumer's interests, to say nothing of those of the local merchant, is thwarted and sacrificed. A perfected societal order, economically speaking, means a perfected functioning, not of individuals, but of economic segments of individuals. Society as our aim is *not* the same as the self-expression of the individual, in spite of all the assertions of our social scientists and institutional leaders to the contrary.

Let us now consider the ethics of the gasoline filling station. I have learned, in motoring, that when my radiator is empty, but my gasoline and oil supply are good, it is wise to stop at the filling station of some great oil company, such, for example, as stations marked Socony. Here one can count on courteous treatment, and even service, regardless of whether one desires to make a purchase or not. A splendid argument, it would seem, in favor of the efficiency of modern big business. But let us look more closely. There are two views of the ethics of helpfulness, according to whether we think of individuals or of organized society. The latter view is that of the business men engaged in the special sale of their gasoline products. They have learned their lesson in human psychology a little better than the slow, old-fashioned grocer, who operates a gasoline pump as an annex to his store. Having found that politeness and service pay, they have established rigorous courses of training for their filling-station attendants, and have required them to develop expertness in the courtesies which

[207]

can be proffered to motorists stopping at their stations. Neighboring stations run by large-scale competitors are also likely to be governed by the same principle. The result of business competition, in other words, seems here to be to increase the general level of politeness and service in business transactions. But a fundamental question now arises. Is the courtesy here involved a characteristic of individuals as personalities, or incident only to economic situations? Will the attendant be polite to his neighbor when he meets him that evening because he has practiced his politeness upon the passing motorists who wanted their radiators filled; or will he have to wait until some business function has absorbed his relationship to his neighbor? Must his neighbor pass by his gasoline station in order to have courtesy and helpfulness extended to him? What is the difference, someone may ask, so long as we increase the number of situations of life in which politeness has become the rule for social conduct? That is a question which everyone must answer for himself. Do we want values which mean nothing to individuals except that they are inseparable components of business transactions; or do we want values which an individual will seek in *every* situation simply because he, as an individual, prizes them? Is the altruistic motive to originate from individuals everywhere no matter what their position, or from a few individuals who are shrewd enough to incorporate it as a part of the technique of selling?[1]

Educational institutions offer a field for similar observations. A parent is sometimes struck by the contrast between the excellent record of deportment on his child's

[1] It should also be noted that service in business as developed in our modern era of competition means really service as a result rather than as a motive. A business man by rendering service to a prospective customer renders a disservice to his competitor by capturing the prospective customer's business for himself. The application of the principle of service through business enterprise can never, therefore, become truly universal, as an attitude of character or personality can.

report card, and the behavior of the same child as a member of the family group. This situation again reflects the opposition between the individual as a unit in social organization, and social organization as a mere expression of the desires of the individual. At school my child is in terror, like many children, of being sent to the principal's office. Yet I am puzzled to know why, for very little happens to a child in the principal's office beyond a few reproving glances or words from a dignified individual who hovers about that place. Perhaps the reason is that behavior at school is but a single segment of the child's life, and is effectively separated in most school systems from his life at home, in his gang, or elsewhere. Control over that one segment can be easily and authoritatively established. By delegating absolute authority in certain matters to school principals, and by requiring uniform school behavior of all children, we can achieve a remarkable degree of prediction and control of the behavior of the child in the school situation. But perhaps this control is unusually effective precisely because the situation is artificially segmental, that is, because it includes only a part of the child as a biological and psychological organism. Once outside this departmental influence, a thousand other tendencies of the child's personality may be released. We may question whether the law-abiding behavior which the child learns as the segment of his life in an educational institution will be transferred to his conduct in life generally. Because administrators desire primarily an orderly and well-run school, some of them lose sight of the objective of producing an orderly and responsible child. The assumption that these two objectives are one and the same thing, or even that the one leads necessarily to the other, is a fallacy as dangerous as it is widely accepted. The same conclusion is suggested by the work of Professors May and Hartshorne, who have found that children in modern city schools do not tend to develop consistent traits of honesty which they reveal in all relationships, but are honest or dishonest according as they have been taught in specific situations.

The conflict between the standard of institutional behavior and individual personality in education is further reflected by the status of family life and its relation to our schools. The ordeal of every parent's life in regard to the school problem seems to center in two inescapable duties: first, to see that the children reach school on time; and secondly, to see that they are clean when they leave home.[2] But when they return home the situation is likely to be very different. They are frequently dirty, and are likely to be tardy, anywhere from fifteen minutes to two hours. Why should teachers not undertake the same responsibility as parents for the training of the children in habits of cleanliness and punctuality? But the overworked teacher at once, and perhaps justly, replies, "Our business is to teach the standardized branches of knowledge, and not to be concerned with moral and personal habits." There is truth on both sides, but the dilemma cannot be escaped. The higher, technical educational standards demanded for our modern, complex civilization, standards which force all the child's training into separate compartments in the interests of efficiency, are directly opposed to the task of helping the child to develop his own character and his own values in all the situations which he meets. Because the lives of children are now being supervised under so many separate segments, the problem of the parent, who seems to be the only one looking out for the child as a complete individual, is becoming increasingly difficult. We expect the average child to be taught habits of punctuality and cleanliness; these are traits which characterize socially desirable individuals. Yet the time and opportunity

[2] For this illustration the writer is indebted to Mrs. Sidonie M. Gruenberg.

for inculcating these habits in our institutionalized society are very limited. No matter how careful and exhausting the parent's efforts in that direction, the training virtually stops between the hours of 9:00 A.M. and 4:00 P.M., while the child is in school. The parent is held responsible for the development of moral and social traits in the child's personality; yet those things which the child may learn while functioning segmentally in the school system may undo the parent's most careful training. Modern life has kept the form or shell of the family relationship, with little or none of its reality as a source of character training.

When we turn to the political field we can again understand many contemporary problems as the conflict between the institutionalist's and the individualist's points of view. The ideal of democratic government in the earlier days of our country was based more nearly upon the complete expression of the desires and interests of individuals. Life seemed to be centered in the local communities, with little control by state or national organization of either an economic or a political type. The policies worked out in these local governments were able to represent more nearly, though of course, not entirely, the wishes of the individuals concerned, and to represent them as individuals and not as classes or pressure groups composed of farmers, manufacturers, trade-union members, or other special segments of interest to which Professor Dewey has given the name publics. The notion of the "right of each *interest* to be represented" in a democracy is an absurdity. An interest is a purely logical abstraction of a segment of life. An interest, being a metaphysical abstraction, has no right; but a human being, as a creature *possessing* interests, has. Try as we may to integrate all of these publics or interests into a society, we have had little success in bringing about a true expression of individual personalities in the affairs of government. We always find that it is the particu-

[211]

lar segment of interest which is represented, and not the individual.

The increasing complexity of technological industry, the rapidity of transportation and communication, the intricacy of incorporated business, have rendered the task of government so difficult that it can be directed only by "experts," and by these only when each is working in a particular subdivision of the field. There has accordingly grown up, as over against the simple historical idea of individual representation, a totally different political philosophy. There has emerged, gradually and unconsciously, the notion that government is more than the behavior of individuals; it is thought of as an institution over and above the individuals. It is a system or a social machine for passing laws and administering justice. This "machinery of government," moreover, has grown to be so complex that we have to employ experts to operate it. No one actually sees the government; but since almost everyone talks about it in this objective fashion, the average man assumes its existence by the suggestion arising from the impression of its universal acceptance. We have, then, on the one hand, the traditional theory that government is the direct voice of all the citizens as individuals, and on the other hand, the notion, much nearer to our practical working philosophy, that government is an agency separated from the people and run for them by experts. It is the bane of politics that, in order to capture votes, we continually pretend to be acting under the former philosophy, when we are really acting under the latter. Many assert, for example, that the Eighteenth Amendment to the Constitution is actually the expression of the will of the individuals of the country. Yet it was in large measure enacted by representatives in different states who were serving at least in part under the conviction that they were experts chosen not merely to represent individuals, but to "run the government." In keeping with the same ideology, the President of the United States has recently set up a special commission of experts to see what should be done now about this vexing question. A stock argument of the wets is "Prohibition can't be enforced." This argument is often illogical as used, because the one who uses it is trying to legislate for everyone else. To be accurate he ought to say frankly, "I don't wish to obey the law and there is probably an undetermined number of people like me. Let us see how many there are." The favorite argument of the drys, "Give prohibition a chance" is likewise illogical, because it substitutes a plan devised by a special group for a true representation of what the individuals of the country want to do about the question. If all who believe in drinking, whether moderate or immoderate, were to acquiesce and truly "give prohibition a chance," of course it would work— for as long as they acquiesced. When the drinkers got tired of acquiescing the scheme would again break down, because, as many of the drys would doubtless allege, it was not being given a chance. This absurd begging of the question on both sides comes from our forgetting that society and government are essentially only individuals after all, and that a social institution, plan, or system which is alleged to be an objective fact, and which is supposed to be something more than the individuals in question, is from the standpoint of scientific investigation, a pure illusion.

There are those who will say that the subtle questions of modern social engineering cannot be settled merely by counting noses. Many will insist that the notion of government as something to be delegated to experts is both necessary and desirable in the complexity of modern life. The answer is simple. It is desirable only in so far as this complexity of modern life is itself desirable. That we do treasure the idea of government as an expression of individuals is shown by the fact that we still appeal to voters in elections upon this basis; and the appeal is effective. But the widening gap between behavior as the spontaneous act of personalities and behavior as institutional alignment and symbol-worship obscures the realities of political action just as it is making increasingly difficult an intelligent approach to industrial, educational, and familial problems.

The same assumption of a separation between individual and societal realities is to be noted in theories of public opinion. Let me quote from a work on social psychology written less than a decade ago.

In the long run the upshot of the process of discussion is the emergence of a new phase in the psychological history of the group: a public opinion. It is more fundamental than the algebraic sum of individual opinions. As excitement is allayed, reflection ensues, and in such instances there is food for reflection for in the initial period of excitement individual opinions, formed at every angle of approach, of every degree of maturity and good sense, have been bandied about, and each wide-awake member of the community has observed many types of reaction thereto. Gradually there emerges, as a result of a slow, but more spontaneous than deliberate analysis, a certain apprehension of common and fundamental interests by all members of the group. This is a public opinion. It has no reference to all the varied contents of consciousness of the individuals who make up a community. It is rather, as we conceive it, a certain resultant that remains over from having entertained many opinions of more or less maturity. It is a sublimation from all that has been stirring individual natures during weeks of campaign commotion; one that has been helped on at many a cross-road and elsewhere by discussion, the genius of which is to sift; and because it is such a sublimation, attained by those elements in the community that are by nature capable of reflection and discussion and disposed thereto, rather than by the unstable cravers for excitement, or by those whose dullness blocks reflection and discussion, it can be safely assumed to touch more fundamental issues, and therefore to lie upon a higher plane than the average opinion or the algebraic sum of the opinions of all individuals in the community.[3]

Such a statement as this seems to imply that out of group discussion there emerges a type of attitude or opinion which is qualitatively different from and superior to that which individuals, prior to their group activity, might attain. This is clearly a matter not for a priori conclusion, but for research. A number of experiments have been performed to ascertain whether, upon a question of fact, a more accurate judgment is derived from the average or consensus of opinion of individuals after they have been members of a discussion group than by taking isolated individual opinion without discussion. The results of these experiments have been somewhat conflicting; but through recent studies we have come to the conclusion, at least tentatively, that the belief in a superior average opinion resulting from group discussion may be justly challenged. It is necessary clearly to distinguish the factors here involved. Let us take, for example, opinion regarding the number of beans in a glass jar, to be estimated without counting. Here is a question of fact upon which the results of group discussion, as over against isolated judgment, can be accurately determined. The following measurements should be kept in mind. First, there is the average judgment of the members of the group regarding the question at issue, the members judging first as isolated individuals before discussion, and then later after a period of group discussion centered about the problem of the number of beans in the jar. A variation of this judgment might be the arriving at an estimate by discussion and compromise, which would not necessarily be the average judgment, but which would be the estimate accepted by all with the least reservation. We now have two group

[3] GAULT, R. H., "Social Psychology," pp. 176–177. Quoted by special permission of the publisher, Henry Holt and Company, and with a slight alteration as directed by the author.

averages, or judgments, namely, one before and one after discussion. Which of these will be likely to differ least from the actual number of beans? By this method we can measure an average individual error before discussion, and a group error after discussion. The comparison of these errors of estimate will give us an indication of whether, in such a simple question of fact as the number of beans in a glass jar, a process of improvement of opinion through group interaction, such as that described in the quotation above, really takes place.

But there is another type of measurement which we should also keep in mind. We can measure the error not for the group average, but for *each individual separately*. Here we shall learn the effect of the discussion upon each individual in the group, what proportion of the individuals improve with discussion, what proportion make still less accurate estimates, and what is the average of the improvement of the individuals who improve as compared with the average increase of error of those whose second estimate is worse than the first. We have, in other words, a possibility of comparing the results of discussion not only in group-wise fashion, as the average or consensus of opinion of the group, but with regard to what the group activity has meant to individuals.

Now the results so far obtained show clearly the importance of distinguishing these two types of measures. For we have found no reliable indication whatsoever that the *average* or *group* opinion is any more accurate after discussion than before. Treating the individuals, therefore, as a group and thinking of the average of their opinion as "public opinion," we cannot say that this judgment is any better than the average of the isolated individual opinions before the so-called public came into existence. On the other hand, if we turn our attention to the number of individuals whose opinions improve or grow worse as a result of group discussion, we see that a decided reduction of the error of estimate has taken place. There are substantially more individuals whose judgments get better as a result of the discussion than there are individuals whose judgments grow worse.[4] Clearly a kind of educational process is taking place, in which the individuals who were previously extreme in their judgments have corrected their estimates through the influence of group members taking a more moderate view. We are met, therefore, by the striking fact that individuals may improve, while the group as such, treated as a mathematical average, does not. In other words, we should be no more inclined to trust the "group judgment," which embodies a supposedly superior "public" opinion, than to accept the average of individual judgments made before the public, as a discussion process, had come into being. On the other hand, after such a process has been under way for a time, we can take at random any *individual* and justly feel a greater assurance in accepting his opinion as coming somewhere near the truth than if we took that individual's opinion before the discussion had taken place. It should be emphasized that we are only in the initial stages of experiment in this field, and the above statement is to be considered as tentative. Such facts, however, as we do possess seem to throw doubt upon the superiority of opinion of a group as such. The group discussion does have a very clear effect; but this effect seems to relate to the character of the judgment of individuals and not to the resultant judgment of the group as a group.[5] Discussion clarifies and informs the responses of

[4] For these experimental facts the writer is indebted to the researches of his present and former graduate students at Syracuse University, particularly those of Dr. Arthur Jenness, Miss Dorothy Loeb, and Mr. Samuel Cummings.

[5] Some readers will object to our drawing an inference in the complex problems of public opinion from so simple an experiment as estimating the number of beans in a glass jar. I concede that our results are suggestive only. There are certain points, however, which can properly be made in defense of this inference. In the

individuals, but it does not, to our knowledge, improve "the mind of a group."

Through studies in social psychology it has been found that opinions and attitudes which we call public are subject to a number of distorting and confusing influences merely because those who hold them regard them as public rather than private opinions. There is, for example, the principle of *pluralistic ignorance*, which accompanies our tendency to assume that the great body called the public *has* a definite intent or wish which the government should carry out. Given the disposition to believe this, the ignorance of each citizen concerning the actual state of belief or desire of most of the other citizens furnishes a background upon which various distortions may occur. In such a pluralistic ignorance one is readily convinced by propaganda, particularly when such propaganda is a projection of the individual's own wishes. That is to say, we accept as "public" opinion that view which we hold ourselves, and

---

first place, our results apply only to questions of fact; that is, to questions upon which there is an ascertainable correct answer which can be used for purposes of checking the errors of estimate. In perhaps the majority of current popular issues there is no such available standard of accuracy. The questions must remain matters of opinion. In this case, obviously, no quantitative experiment is possible. We must remain in ignorance as to whether the consensus or group average is better than that arrived at by individuals in isolation. This limitation, of course, would invalidate both any negative statement and any positive eulogy of the public opinion process such as that given in the quotation above. We can experiment only with factual questions. Regarded in this light, our bean experiment seems to be much more of a kind with questions of fact involved in public issues; and the hypothesis we have suggested may seem to be fairly reasonable. There are two other cautions, however, that must be borne in mind. If the so-called public contains one or more experts who know the facts, then it will not take them long to convince their fellows of their superior knowledge, and so greatly improve the consensus of group judgment. The other reservation relates to the discovery, not of objective facts, but of the existence of common interests which can be revealed fully only through discussion. In either of these situations our experimental hypothesis does not apply. But it may be also said that these instances do not cover more than a part of that which is generally included in the term public opinion, as will be seen in fact from the quotation we have been discussing.

[218]

would like other people to hold. Another attitude that comes into the picture is the desire to *conform* to the rest of the group, the aversion, in other words, to appearing or to being atypical. It has been found that subjects who are working alone, but with their work period controlled by signals which also control other subjects in other rooms, will show, to some extent, the same effects upon their work that would occur if others were actually present and working with them. A situation of this sort, no doubt, arises when a man or woman goes into a voting booth. The presence of other voters in neighboring booths or in the voting station may tend to make the individual conform with what he thinks to be the mode of the opinion of the group. Through public opinion as a psychological attitude, rather than through public opinion as a fact, a definite control is exerted over the responses of the voter.

One of the problems which has troubled civic leaders is the indifference of people generally to the serious duties of citizenship, particularly with reference to participation in party primaries, civic organizations, and elections. A careful study has recently been conducted at the University of Chicago upon reasons for not voting. From the standpoint of the present discussion, it would seem to be a little more promising to conduct a study on reasons *for* voting. Non-voting, rather than voting, is the result we should naturally expect from the institutionalization of behavior in the political field. Where only one segment of activity is involved the individual is not greatly interested, unless, as in clear-cut economic issues, the rest of his life hangs upon the successful functioning of that one segment. This inevitable lack of interest in institutionalized politics is accompanied by the fiction of a personified institution known as the government. Whether this fiction of a government over the heads of individuals be a sincere conviction or a rationalization for nonparticipation, the individual who holds it

[219]

will probably see little reason for voting. He will be likely to take little interest in the minute and perfunctory, almost ritualistic, part which he is expected to play. An important experiment, therefore, for getting at the psychological basis of political indifference will be a future study of the popular ideology concerning government and the relation of such ideology to the participation or nonparticipation of citizens.

The problems of law enforcement and crime provide another field in which our hypothesis may be tested. What is law in psychological terms? Is it really true that a violation of one law will be likely to lead to violations of other laws? This is a statement dogmatically made by the heads of our so-called legal and political institutions. Whether it is true, I think, depends upon whether the individual law-breaker thinks of law as a detached symbol, or an institution separate from himself, toward which, as toward a being, he may be hostile or friendly, toward which he may show either reverence or contempt. If this is his ideology, the "all or none" formula may apply; that is, disregard of one law may lead to disrespect toward law in general. On the other hand, if the individual thinks of law as that which the majority of citizens do, or wish to be done, he will feel free to change his behavior in respect to obedience whenever he has evidence that the majority may wish to behave differently. And this attitude need not necessarily affect his obedience to other laws, that is, to law in general. Certain abuses will of course arise through rationalizations concerning the supposed attitude of the majority. But such rationalizations are perhaps no worse than those which are employed by the advocates of a transcendental view of law, who seek to control individual action through the symbol of a legal institution above the heads of the people. Here again, is a fruitful field for psychological investigation. A research upon this question would no doubt reveal a number of hitherto unrecognized processes of social control.

The appalling prevalence of crime in present-day America, while its roots are complex, can, I think, be partly explained by this conflict between the individual as a unique personality and his institutional habits. There is an intimate connection between modern graft, racketeering, and gang rule on the one hand and our economic organization upon the other. In the older days when a person's wealth consisted largely of what he had in his house or could carry about, robbery was a more intimate and personal affair. The robber simply met his victim in a dark alley, struck him down, and took away his money. There was in these encounters, if we may be permitted the expression, an inclusion of the total individual. One individual met another in a face-to-face manner and deprived him of his fortune. Holdups are, of course, by no means out of date; but because such events are spectacular and deal with acts in which the whole individual as an organism is involved, there is a possibility of bringing them fairly well under control. Even with the modern automobile this kind of crime would not represent more than a comparatively small portion of the predatory activities of our modern society. When, as nowadays, robbery can be committed, not as a person-to-person affair, but through a network of institutional habits, involving often the economic life of an entire city, the possibilities for its exploitation are indefinitely multiplied, and the opportunity to check it is correspondingly small. The strictly up-to-date and efficient brigand does not snatch away Smith's money and then disappear from the scene. Instead, he gears himself in as a part of the economic institution. By means of power at the physical level, he levies a tribute upon the economic activities of merchant Smith, a tribute which ultimately must be paid by Mr. Smith's customers, that is, eventually, by the people of the city at large. Racketeering, so far as its

[221]

behavior pattern is concerned, is not greatly different from the legitimate collection of taxes by city officials. In the latter case, of course, a different group of persons collect the taxes and use them, at least in part, for more social ends. The penalties for failure to pay are also somewhat less summary and drastic. But in both cases the tribute gathering is worked in as a functional part of the behavior which makes up our economic institutions. Here again, the trouble lies in the fact that we have organized life on a basis of segments of behavior common to everybody, yet fully representing nobody, segments which we set up as the institutions of our economic and social order. In preying upon human activities it is, therefore, unnecessary to deal with whole individuals as such. One needs to deal only with the agencies or centers from which the institutional habits of a large number of people can be controlled and manipulated. The individual organism disappears and the societal organism seems to take its place. Crime of this type is no longer the profiting of individual A by the exploiting of individual B, but the success of A in getting control of the machine we call society. It seems likely that the criminal tendency in mankind as individuals is no greater today than in earlier years; but the possibility of its successful pursuit has, through institutional behavior, been considerably enlarged.

In international relations the chasm between the individual viewpoint and the societal concept is no less clearly marked. Here again, we can look at the world as a collection of individual human personalities, each differing from the others, or we can view it as an array of organized groups to which historians and publicists have given the name of nations. If we take the former view the problem of international warfare disappears. If we take the latter view, such warfare is likely to continue; for nationalistic groupings have sprung up and have been strengthened in part for the very purpose of concerted struggle and for advantage to the individuals so associated. It is interesting to note the manner in which the national representatives in the League of Nations regard their activity. Are they spokesmen of *nations*, as collections of partially inclusive segments of common interest, or of *individuals*, that is, of whole and unique personalities, who live within designated geographical boundaries. If they are representatives of the latter type, they can talk more freely to one another around the Council table; while if they regard themselves as the spokesmen of nations, they are limited to the expression of certain common interests, policies, and traditions treated as defining the will of the nation concerned. Here again is the old conflict in international form. We can view the inhabitants of the world as whole individuals, on the one hand, or deal with them, on the other, as standardized units of thought, action, and feeling, whose responses are dictated by the nature of the groupings to which they belong. One of our most important tasks in social psychology is the development of scales and techniques for studying national and racial attitudes, and for measuring allegiance—or hostility—to institutional fictions and stereotypes of nation, race, and class. Experiments measuring the effect of propaganda upon international attitudes, as well as the effect of institutional thinking upon individual behavior, are already under way.

III

What I am offering here, for the field of the social problems, is not an application of psychology with clearcut techniques and measurable results, such as we are familiar with in industry, medicine, law, and other pursuits. My task has to do with a more difficult and intangible problem. Psychology cannot be applied to social and political problems in the same way in which it can be

[223]

applied to any of the recognized industries or professions. For in the latter the objects to be achieved are taken for granted. In social problems, however, the ends themselves are often vague and little understood. When we accept institutional behavior and standards as fixed, the problem of the means for enforcing them is relatively simple; when, however, we wish to examine the justification for our institutions themselves, we cannot escape the deeper problem of the life-values by which they must be judged. The present issue, therefore, cannot be separated from the search for and realization of a philosophy of life, and our task is to bring to the service of such a quest whatever help psychological analysis and experiment can offer.

In the midst of the complexity of present-day life it is difficult for us to see the demarcation between these two fields, the individual and the institutional, into which behavior is being directed. If we could place ourselves at a greater distance from the human scene, these broad features might become a little more distinct; just as the details of a piece of country are more intelligible to the aeroplane observer than to one who travels through it on foot. Suppose that a scientist were to come to the earth from Mars in order to make observations.[6] Let us suppose that we have taken him to a tower near the intersection either of two country roads or of two streets, at the outskirts of New York City. He would now see automobiles coming from any one or more of four directions. As the automobiles approached the intersection he would observe various changes—stopping, acceleration, or deceleration—in their movement, from which, if he knew anything about terrestial mechanisms, he would infer corresponding types of behavior on the part of their drivers. Should two cars be approaching the intersection at the same time from direc-

---

[6] The following illustration is a modification of one originally proposed in a master's thesis written by Milton Dickens.

[224]

tions at right angles to each other, he would see that one car would slow down or stop long enough to allow the other car to pass. Which car would stop and which would pass through would depend probably upon a number of factors, for example, their relative nearness to the intersection, or their relative speed, which factors might in turn be related, directly or indirectly, to the temperaments of the particular drivers. The instances of stopping or accelerating might also depend upon such characteristics of the drivers as their relative degrees of aggressiveness or submissiveness, haste or leisure, politeness or impoliteness, and the like. There would be no outside, "institutional" influence determining what should be done, but only the circumstances of time and place and the personality traits of the individuals involved. The cars, in other words, would behave toward one another very much as human beings behave in their informal, face-to-face relationships.

Should the Martian observer desire to be more accurate in his observations, he could make a chart of the frequency of starting, stopping, or going of the automobiles observed. He would probably find, if he did this, that the behavior of the cars, that is, the behavior of the individuals driving them, would be distributed in the form of what is familiarly known as the bell-shaped curve of normal probability. This result is to be expected from the manner in which human traits or capacities are distributed in an unselected population. Taking, for example, the trait of ascendance-submission, let us think of persons arranged along a scale from the most aggressive on the one extreme, to the most retiring and self-effacing upon the other. Experiments with tests of this trait have shown that by far the greater number of people are neither extremely ascendant nor extremely submissive, but are in the middle region of the scale. As we go out from this middle region toward the ascendant extreme, we find a decreasing number of

[225]

individuals, until we come to the most ascendant individual of the group, who stands practically alone at the extreme of the scale. On the other side of the mid-region we find people decreasing in number toward the most submissive extreme. The measurement of any trait of personality, as well as measurements of intelligence, body weight, stature, or any other biological or psychological characteristic seem to give us this same bell-shaped form of distribution. We may call this the natural biological or psychological distribution. It is unmodified thus far by any sweeping artificial, cultural, or social influence, such as a law, a custom, or an economic process. In the Martian observer's record we should expect to find that the motorists who have a *moderate* degree of some trait expressed in driving are in the large majority; and this moderate possession of the trait will dictate their action. That is, they will neither rush in, nor will they hang back and stop altogether; they will be more likely to slacken their pace and proceed somewhat cautiously. Only a few of the bolder ones will push through without slowing up, and only a few of the more timid or polite will stop altogether. We should, therefore, expect to find reflected in this free, non-institutionalized traffic situation the probability curve of normal distribution. It is also evident that most of the motorists concerned would be reacting in a way natural to them *as individuals* under the circumstances. They would be in a sense expressing their personalities in their encounters with fellow motorists. The task of driving an automobile under these conditions would incline toward our definition of total, rather than partial, inclusion.

Now suppose that we remove our Martian observer from the rural districts to the corner of Fifth Avenue and Thirty-third Street, New York City, and place him on the top of the Empire State Building. Looking down upon this scene, if he had never been closer to the earth than the roof of the building in question, he might suppose that he was observing a different species of vehicle from those he had witnessed at the country crossroads. Instead of reacting as man to man, the drivers of the cars would seem to be scarcely aware of one another at all, but would all start or stop together as if by some kind of magic. If the Martian had an inkling of what earth-beings, with their stimulus-response mechanisms, were like, he might guess the truth, namely, that they were responding not to one another, but to some common controlling stimulus which he would be too far from the earth to see or hear. Should he make records from this vantage point for purposes of comparison, we should expect that the distribution of behavior would be of a different type from that observed in the uncontrolled traffic situation of the country crossroads. In the *traffic-signal* situation, the observer from Mars might measure the frequency with which motorists arriving at a given corner when the signal was against them obeyed that signal and stopped, and the frequency with which they passed through in disregard of the signal, checking their speed only slightly or not at all. In this case we should expect that the mode of the curve (that is, the greatest frequency), instead of being at the mid-region, representing, say a moderate, cautious slackening of speed, would be at the extreme end of the scale. That is, most of the motorists would come to a complete stop when the signal was against them. Regardless of varying individual degrees of boldness or timidity, hurry or leisure, politeness or rudeness, the great mass of drivers would stop when faced by the red signal. Conformity to this extreme of behavior, demanded by law under threat of punishment, would therefore probably be high. There would be relatively few whose personal traits were so impelling that they would run through when the signal was adverse. A few might go through after slowing up and looking about to observe whether another

[227]

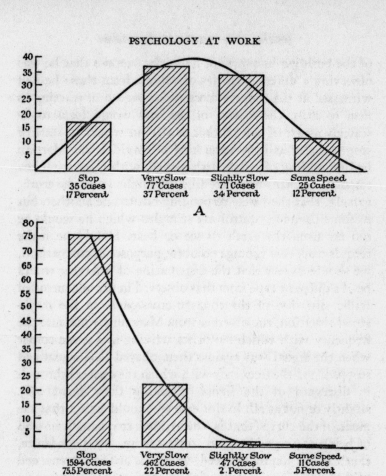

Fig. 1.—*A.* Distribution of behavior of 208 motorists at a corner where there was cross traffic, but no traffic signals. As each motorist crossed the corner, his behavior was classified into one of four catagories: (1) those coming to a stop; (2) those crossing at very slow speed; (3) those crossing at a slightly slower speed; and (4) those crossing with no apparent alteration of speed. These four categories are indicated at the bottom of the proper columns. The height of the columns shows the percentage of subjects whose reaction fell within the limits of each of the four units on the scale. These data were gathered in Syracuse, New York, on a corner where there were no traffic signals of any kind, but every subject was reacting to cross traffic, *i.e.*, other cars crossing the corner from other directions at about the same time. *B.* Distribution of behavior of 2,114 motorists at corners where there were both cross traffic and boulevard stop signs. The four steps on the scale are the same as described above. These data were gathered on corners in Syracuse, New York, and Los Angeles, California.

[228]

car was approaching or a policeman was in sight, and fewer still, the very boldest, might rush through without changing their speed. We should expect, however, that the distribution of these atypical individuals would follow a rapidly declining proportion, so that the curve, instead of being a normal, bell-shaped one, would be J-shaped, having its mode at one extreme of the scale (that is, at the complete stop), and rapidly descending in frequency toward the mid-region of the scale. There is in the traffic-signal situation but very little opportunity for expressing individual differences of temperament on the part of the drivers, whereas in the uncontrolled traffic movement, we have seen that there would be a maximum opportunity for the revealing of such differences. The viewpoint under which the traffic control system is conceived is that of partial rather than total inclusion. All efforts are made to establish only *one* segment of response in the entire population, deviations from this mode of behavior being made as rare as possible.

Let us abandon our fictitious Martian observer and talk about realities. The hypothesis which has just been presented has been put to the test by Milton C. Dickens, who has observed and recorded thousands of instances of the actual behavior of motorists under varying conditions. We present here some of his results. The upper diagram of Fig. 1 shows the distribution of the behavior of 208 motorists observed at a certain street intersection in Syracuse, New York. At this corner there were buildings obscuring the motorists' view from every direction; but there was no traffic signal of any kind, either traffic light or boulevard stop sign. The behavior of the motorists was recorded only in cases where traffic was approaching the intersection on the other street at the same time. What the motorists did on these occasions was observed on a four-step scale, the positions of which were, respectively:

[229]

1. Complete stop
2. Slowing down to a very slow speed
3. Slackening the pace slightly
4. Going ahead without any alteration of speed

The height of the column erected upon each step indicates the percentage of the entire group falling on that step of the scale. I have drawn through the centers of the tops of these columns a curved line which suggests what we might expect the distribution to be if the steps of our scale were more finely differentiated and our number of cases sufficiently great.[7] It will be seen that there is here some evidence for our hypothesis of a normal, bell-shaped curve of distribution where a purely individual, rather than an institutionalized, situation is presented.

The lower curve of this figure is based upon 2,114 cases, and includes not only the general location already mentioned in Syracuse, but certain street crossings in Los Angeles, California. The situation in these cases also involved the presence of approaching traffic; but in addition to this every motorist whose behavior was tabulated was faced by a boulevard stop sign. While keeping the presence of opposed traffic constant as a uniform condition, we are thus measuring the effect of a particular variable, namely, a sign placed at an intersection by municipal officials, commanding the driver to stop before crossing. The results are

[7] It should be pointed out, however, that the scale here employed, as well as others used in this study were only rough, a priori, logical scales. In order to have a scale in the true sense, that is, with steps known to be equal, it will be necessary to construct it in accordance with some special technique, such for example as the psychophysical procedures suggested by Professor L. L. Thurstone. This construction of a telic or logical scale for the measurement of institutional behavior will be the next step in the research. For the present, however, it may be said that the rough scales here used do at least suggest that the hypothesis of distribution we have advanced may be true. A change in the scale value of the positions as worded might skew the curve, but would still leave it with a tendency toward the normal type. No serious disturbance in the curve would be likely, since it is fairly certain that the steps of our scale are, at least, in the correct order.

[230]

very different from those shown in the upper half of the figure. Whereas only 17 per cent of the motorists in the free situation stopped completely, 75.5 per cent of those faced by the traffic sign came to a full stop. The two middle steps of

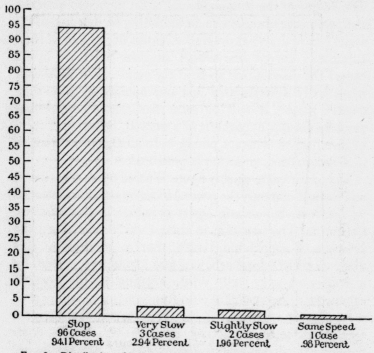

Fig. 2.—Distribution of behavior of 102 motorists at a corner with red lights and a policeman, but without cross traffic. Each of the subjects in this experiment was in the front row of traffic and was not constantly confronted by cross traffic. Thus, as far as other cars were concerned, each of these subjects *might* have crossed the corner without waiting for the signal. The only things preventing such a crossing were the red lights and the policeman. The four steps on the scale are the same as described in A, Fig. 1. The data were gathered in Syracuse, New York.

the scale, which in the free situation drew 37 and 34 per cent respectively, are in the stop-sign situation represented by only 22 and 2 per cent. Out of the entire 2,114 cases there were only one half of 1 per cent who proceeded at full speed, in complete disregard of the sign. The mode has thus shifted to the left extreme of the scale; and the curve instead of being normal in character has become like the letter J (or rather the reverse of the letter J) in form.

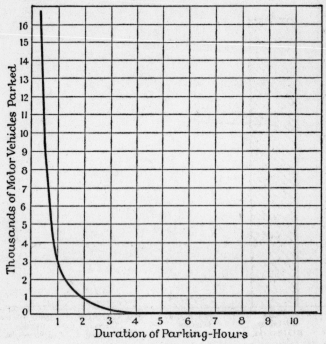

FIG. 3.—Distribution of behavior of several thousand motorists in various districts of Kansas City, showing length of time their cars remained parked.

If we consider situations in which the stimulus is not a constant stop sign, obedience to which often seems so arbitrary a matter, but red and green traffic lights, we find that the tendency of the curve to become J-shaped is more marked. Figure 2 is based upon the observation of 102 cases at the crossing of Fayette and Salina Streets in Syracuse (perhaps the most congested corner of that city), an intersection whose traffic was regulated by policemen working in conjunction with the traffic lights. The observations were made for half an hour at the noon period. Since cars in a row stopping for a light block one another, the results were recorded only for cars approaching the inter-

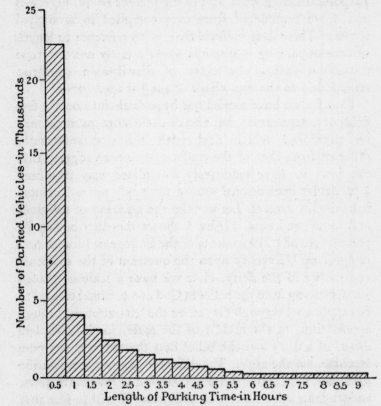

FIG. 4.—Distribution of behavior of several thousand motorists in various districts of Detroit, showing length of time their cars remained parked.

section *alone* or as the *first* car in a row. Hence the driver of the car tabulated was free to disregard the signal if he chose. A glance at Fig. 2 will show that the uniformity of behavior here was very marked. Of the 102 cases, 96 fell on the extreme end of the scale representing "Stop"; while

[233]

3, 2, and 1 cases, respectively, failed to stop and violated the signal in progressive degree.

Other records concerning obedience to traffic ordinances have been tabulated and put in graphic form for practical purposes different from that of the present study. Figures 3 and 4 are reproduced from data compiled in municipal studies.[8] These data indicate that, with reference to length of time of parking in districts where a fairly uniform time restriction exists, the curve of distribution conforms remarkably to the hypothesis of the J-shaped curve.

Thus far we have carried our hypothesis into only a few fields of investigation; but two or three more instances may be mentioned which deal with behavior sufficiently different from that of the traffic situation to suggest that the law we have tentatively formulated may transcend a particular institutional setting and apply to institutional behavior in general. Let us take the question of religious and moral attitudes. Figure 5 shows the distribution by percentages of 1,219 students of the College of Liberal Arts in Syracuse University upon the question of the existence and nature of the deity. Here we have a scale of graded steps, ranging from the belief in God as a personal creator to be supplicated through prayer, on the left extreme, through agnosticism, in the middle of the scale, to the complete denial of a deity and the belief that the universe is a pure machine, on the right. The different groups shown in the figure are, from top to bottom, Catholics, Protestants, Jews, and students with no church affiliation. It will be seen that in the first of these groups, and perhaps to some extent in the second, religious beliefs tend to conform to an institu-

[8] Figure 3 is taken from "A Traffic Control Plan for Kansas City," p. 150, a study by the Albert Russel Erskine Bureau of Harvard University, Miller McClintock, Director. Figure 4 is taken from an article entitled Downtown Storage Garages, by Hawley S. Simpson, *Annals of the American Academy of Political and Social Science*, September, 1927, p. 83. These figures are reproduced by special permission.

tional pattern. Where large numbers of individuals have
been influenced by some common stimulus or teaching, as in

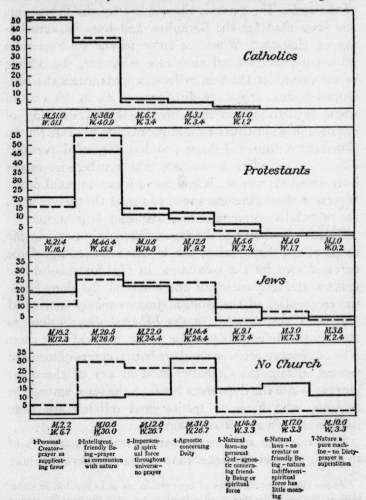

Fig. 5.—Distribution of percentages of 1,219 students of the College of Liberal
Arts of Syracuse University upon the question of the existence and nature of the
deity. (*Reproduced from "Students' Attitudes," by Daniel Katz and Floyd H. Allport.*)

the Catholic faith, we find the characteristic J-shaped
distribution of attitudes. The mode is that of the behavior

or belief held proper within that institution, other attitudes decreasing in frequency as one goes toward the other side of the scale. The curve is skewed less for the Protestants and Jews than for the Catholics, and loses its actual J-shaped character. When we come to the students who profess no institutional allegiance whatever, the outline of the curve, for the men at least, approximates the bell-shaped normal frequency distribution. As in the case of traffic regulation, tendency toward the stereotyping of response in an institutionalized population has thrown the distribution into a J-shape and has concealed personal differences of religious attitude which otherwise might have found expression. Where no such institutional factor is present these differences tend to reveal themselves upon the probability curve of normal frequency distribution.[9]

This fact is shown in the present instance not only by the shape of the distribution, but by the relationship of the curves drawn for the two sexes. In Fig. 5 the solid line denotes the frequencies of the men and the dotted line the frequencies of the women. Just as purely individual differences are obscured in the J-shaped distribution, so also are the differences peculiar to sex. We find that there is less difference between the distribution curves of men and women among the Catholics than in any of the other groups; while the differences between the sexes among the students who have no institutional religion are more marked than in any other group.[10]

Since religious and moral questions involve standards of thinking and feeling, rather than outward behavior, it may

[9] Rather striking confirmations of these results are to be found in an earlier work of Professor Thurstone, dealing however not with the same but with a closely related question—namely attitude toward the Church. See Thurstone and Chave, "The Measurement of Attitude," p. 70, University of Chicago Press, 1929.

[10] For a more complete account of these researches the reader is referred to "Students' Attitudes," by Daniel Katz and Floyd H. Allport, Craftsman Press, Syracuse, New York, 1931.

[236]

be maintained, with some justice, that upon such questions there may be a double set of attitudes or opinions, one set representing what the individuals express publicly, that is, as a part of their institutional relationships, and the other revealing their private or purely personal opinion. If this is true, we might expect a J-shaped curve of attitude distribution for public attitudes, and another curve approaching the normal type for free expression of individual personality differences. Richard Schanck has been working upon this problem in a rural community of three or four hundred inhabitants. He asked his subjects to react for him upon scales representing, among other things, their attitudes toward baptism and card playing. The scales were given in two different ways, representing respectively the situations of public and private opinion. First, the investigator asked the subject (who belonged, for example, to the Methodist Church) to check the behavior or opinion which he deemed proper for himself as a member of that Church. In the second procedure the same individual was asked to check the scale according to his own private feelings. The steps of the scale on card playing were briefly, as follows:

1. I will not play card games of any kind.
2. I will not play games with face cards (but will play flinch, rook, etc.).
3. I will not gamble (but will play any kind of cards for amusement).
4. I will play any kind of cards, whether for money or otherwise.

Figure 6 shows the frequency distribution by percentages on these scales for the two types of attitude, public and private, respectively. It will be seen that in the group of fifty-two Methodists to whom the scale was given, the overwhelming majority for the public attitude fell upon willingness to play card games only so long as the cards used were not regular playing cards. These people, publicly speaking, were flinch and rook players. This attitude in fact corresponded pretty closely to their public behavior. A visitor at one of the community bridge parties in this village would have been surprised to find a small group of Methodists and Baptists in the corner playing rook or flinch, instead of auction. When their private attitudes

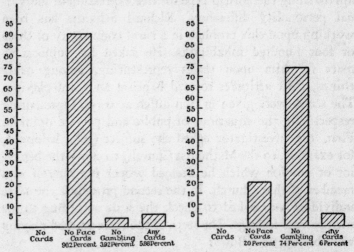

FIG. 6.—Distribution of attitudes toward card playing among church members of a small rural town. The distribution on the left shows the subjects' public attitudes. The distribution on the right shows the private attitudes of the same group of subjects.

were sought, however, the large majority showed a more moderate choice, with the mode falling upon the conviction that it was permissable to play with any cards so long as gambling was not involved. Here again, we find the suggestion of the normal probability distribution of free individual choice, as contrasted with the J-shaped distribution of institutional behavior.

A similar situation is shown in Fig. 7 with regard to the attitude of the Methodists of the town toward baptism.

[238]

A cardinal dispute between the Methodists and the Baptists of this particular town, a controversy which had long stood in the way of a much-needed union of the two churches, was the old question of whether baptism should be by sprinkling or by complete immersion. The two parts of Fig. 7 show the distribution of the public and private attitudes of the Methodists toward this supposedly vital question. When approached as members of an institution,

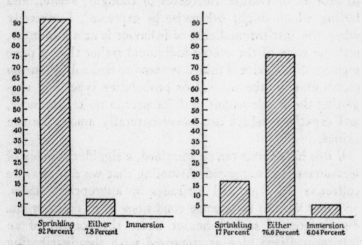

FIG. 7.—Distribution of attitudes toward baptism among methodists in a small rural town. The distribution on the left shows the subjects' public attitudes. The distribution on the right shows the private attitudes of the same group of subjects.

over 90 per cent of Methodists insisted upon the method of sprinkling, 8 per cent consented to either method, and no one preferred immersion. When privately questioned, however, 70 per cent said that either method was acceptable, according to the feeling of the convert. The remainder, who had any personal attitude on the question, were distributed upon either side of this mode.

While these data are only suggestive, they contain a hint of a method which can be used to study institutions and their relation to various social problems. We have shown that when the leaders of the social order look at a part of the individual only, that is, at his reaction as a unit in an economic, political, religious, or educational scheme, the leadership which they attempt to exert in that society will be likely to throw the behavior of the individuals into the skewed or J-shaped distribution. This viewpoint of institutional management and control will also be likely to obscure individual differences of thought, action, and feeling which might otherwise be expressed. Conversely when the institutionalizing of behavior is at a minimum, and the view of the whole individual rather than a mere segment of behavior is taken, we tend to find a distribution conforming to the normal or probability type, and suggesting the whole gamut of differences in traits, attitudes, and capacities which are found naturally among human beings.

If this hypothesis can be sustained, a significant index of measurement is suggested. Assuming that we can measure collective behavior and attitudes by appropriate scales, and that we can so arrange conditions as to discover the distribution of such behavior under the control of an institutionalized plan as compared with the distribution in a non-institutionalized aggregate of people, we can then arrive at a quantitative statement of the discrepancy between these two viewpoints as reflected in the issue concerned. A glance at Fig. 8 will show the theoretical possibilities of such an index. Let curve A represent the complete regulation of certain behavior from the institutional standpoint, and curve B represent behavior having the same function or purpose for adjustment, but subjected to no institutional control. For example, curve A might denote the distribution on a mechanical traffic light system, and curve B the distribution of behavior on meeting vehicles at a country crossroad. Now an index might be devised by appropriate calculations to show the steepness of the slope of the J-shaped curve or the distance between the median of the J-shaped distribution (*a* in Fig. 8) and the median of the normal distribution (*b* in Fig. 8). This slope

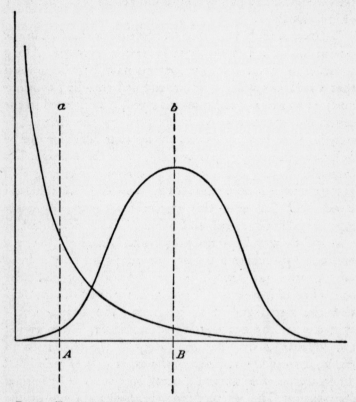

Fig. 8.—Two theoretical behavior distributions and their medians. Distribution *A* is J-shaped; distribution *B* is normal. The dotted lines *a* and *b* represent the medians of the two distributions.

or distance might be taken as an index of the institutionalization of the behavior under consideration. Various types of social organization and control might then be compared on the basis of their discrepancy from normal distribution,

[241]

as indicated by the size of this index. If the coefficient of institutionalization in plan X were greater than that in plan Y, then, other things being equal, X would not be as desirable as Y, because it would not allow free play for the biological and psychological differences of the majority of individuals.

We have already seen some recognition of this fact in the establishment of more flexible traffic systems. Along stretches of boulevard light systems have been so devised that a motorist starting at one end and traveling continuously at an average and constant speed, may proceed to the other end without being interrupted by the changes of signals. Even here, however, we see that behavior can be individualized only approximately, or on the average. The man who is slow and easy-going by temperament, as well as the one who seeks a release of his tensions in a heightened speed, will find even this system inadequate. A newer type of traffic signal, which I believe is being developed, is one which acts in a truly individual manner. When a motorist approaches a corner, his car passes over a tread which turns the signal, in the direction perpendicular to his line of travel, red. When he has crossed the intersection the signal goes back to green. This device would approximate the free meeting of motorists. While giving the advantages of order and safety in the regulation of traffic, it would permit also of the expression of individual differences as they naturally occur on the curve of normal distribution. The Martian observer, looking down on the crossroads, might be observing the effects of such a traffic system without knowing it, since the behavior of the individuals would seem similar at a distance to their behavior if no system at all were present. In such a case the coefficient of institutionalization would approach zero. The same reasoning might be applied with good effect to proposed systems for the regulation of the consumption of alcoholic liquors. If we could find the mode and distribution of natural, uncontrolled behavior in the population upon this question, we could measure the discrepancy between that distribution and the present, probably poorly defined, J curve enforced upon the population under the present law. A scale representing the degree of permanence of the marriage relation in this country as compared with Russia might reveal another interesting and instructive comparison.

Another problem involved in the measurement of institutionalism is that of the relative importance of any one segment of institutional behavior in the whole life of the individual. Some means of measuring this phase of the situation is desirable. Habits of card playing, or even habits of driving in traffic, no matter how institutionalized, do not necessarily involve a large part of the lives of individuals. But if there were associated with these habits others which also follow the J-shaped distribution, the amount of the individual's life which would conform to institutional patterns, as over against normal individual differences, would increase. Consider, for example, the view of the Catholic students at Syracuse University regarding the deity. This one element of their ideational and emotional life may not in itself be important; but if it is correlated with conformist behavior on many other matters, such for example, as the freedom of speech, the limitation of marriage, sex customs, political allegiance, and birth control, then the institutional, J-shaped distribution of attitudes toward the deity becomes highly significant. Such a state of affairs would yield an index of institutionalization not of a population in regard to a particular segment, but of an individual in his whole, or in a large part of, his personality. Some method is needed for measuring this clustering of institutional habits. An example of this, in the older institutional terminology, would be the earlier fusion of Church and State. The separation of the control of these segments, political and religious, is an ideal toward which democratic peoples have long striven. We are perhaps not so clear in recognizing the same problem today in the *economic* institutionalization which now ramifies into fields of education, art, applied science, family life, recreations, and even religion.

IV

In order to understand the contrast between the individual and the institutionalized program in the field of economics, let us compare economic life in a society based upon total inclusion of individuals with that in our own society which is operated upon economic behavior segments almost exclusively. Malinowski has given a good account of the former type of society in his description of the Trobriand Islanders, a people living on an archipelago just north of Australia. The islanders living on the shore are fishers; those who live inland are agriculturists. A division of labor and exchange of products occurs between the two. There is, however, no regular market employing a pecuniary medium of exchange, as in our society. Each fisherman, instead, has established a trading relationship with a certain farmer who brings his garden produce from the interior on stated occasions. No money is passed; there is simply a direct exchange of fish for vegetables or fruits, to the mutual satisfaction of the two parties involved. Quantities exchanged vary according to the conditions of fishing or the crops. Where there is a poor catch or a bad harvest due allowance is made by the other partner in the trade. Only deliberate stinginess and laziness are penalized. It is clear that in a situation of this sort numerous and varied needs, desires, and traits of individuals come into direct contact in the business of economic exchange. Every circumstance about the individual can

[244]

have potentially, at least, a bearing upon the transaction. The situation approaches total inclusion; and the behavior, if we could plot it, would probably resemble in its distribution that of the normal frequency curve of probability. There is here little possibility of overproduction, for if fish are unusually plentiful, there is no incentive for securing a larger catch than necessary. The fisherman would have nothing to gain, for there would be no possibility of amassing monetary profits. His needs for agricultural produce would be quite as well supplied if he secured only a normal catch. The only result, therefore, of a prosperous fishing trip would be that he would not have to work so long to secure his living. He will be unemployed for a considerable part of the time. But this unemployment will not represent suffering for himself or his family; it will merely give an opportunity to do other things in which he is interested, or simply to loaf. In short, in a system of economic exchange which is uninstitutionalized, and which involves the whole person rather than merely a pecuniary segment of his behavior, our present serious problems of overproduction, unemployment, and business depression would be impossible. There would also be no occasion for underproduction, hoarding, or speculation, for nothing could be gained by speculation in a society where prices, profits and dividends on invested capital were unknown.

If we compare with this simple, face-to-face situation our present complex society, we see that in the latter tremendous dislocations between needs and the satisfactions of those needs are not only possible, but likely. Business has become a matter not merely of the fulfillment of wants, but of the stimulation of new wants, the increase of sales, and the accumulation of profits. The manufacturer and merchant cast their products upon a market, hoping for the highest monetary reward they can get. If they can stimulate the buying segment of the people's behavior and increase sales, so much the better, for this will mean higher profits. And profits represent not the direct satisfaction of their own biological needs and personal desires, but a monetary surplus which can be used, both through increased consumption and through further capitalization, to accelerate segmented business activities just so much more. But let us not forget that this philosophy is founded upon only a segment of human behavior and not upon the whole individual. The purpose is to get business operating upon as rapid and high a level as possible. Business behavior is stimulated at the expense of other interests of the organism, and often regardless of genuine needs of many individuals involved in the process. What we need is a closer study of the relation between the economic segment of behavior and the complete life of the normal individual. A curve of normal distribution for the consumption of goods might perhaps be expected in a society where individual needs, traits, and differences alone determined the consumption. As compared with this distribution, it may be possible that through modern business, in which we attempt to standardize economic responses and to persuade each family to buy as many different types of goods and mechanical equipment as possible, we are skewing the curve or even producing a J-shaped distribution. The dislocation between these two curves of behavior—the coefficient, in other words, of the consumer's institutionalism—might throw light upon the problems of overproduction and business depression which now face us. We might tentatively advance the hypothesis that cycles of depression result from these periods of over-accentuation of institutionalized economic behavior. When the skewing of the curve reaches a certain point, or becomes J-shaped, that is, when business as an institution is most flourishing, then the individual organisms rebel. Fear is set up, desire for security is aroused, and people tend to swing back to a condition in which each

[246]

man or woman, as an individual, and in defiance of adver-
tisers and salesmen, determines his or her own standard of
consumption. The causes of business depression may
perhaps lie in this discrepancy between the curves of
economic behavior under an institutional as contrasted
with an individual plan.

The unemployment now prevalent is probably also due
in no small part to the invention of labor-saving machinery. Such machines enable entrepreneurs to produce more
goods and services with the help of fewer hands and brains,
and therefore with a reduction of costs. Many workers are
directly replaced by machinery and new scientific processes
of manufacture. An indirect relationship is the lowering
of the purchasing power of these unemployed considered
as consumers, the consequent slackening of business, and
the throwing of still more men out of work. In view of this
fact we must view somewhat cautiously the widely
prevalent policy of using psychological methods to find the
best possible adjustment between the worker and his
work. So long as the main criterion for that adjustment is
increased economic production, larger profits, and higher
wages, personnel work in factories is really only another
method for accelerating the already exaggerated business
segment of human activity.

If we start again from our assumption of a normal distribution of capacities among workers, we find a conflict arising
in a machine industrialism similar to the conflict between
normal and institutional distributions in the traffic situation. Native capacities for work, such as speed, deftness,
endurance, and the like, seem to be normally distributed.
Yet as the process of manufacture becomes institutionalized,
that is, as we give our main attention to the efficiency of
production rather than to the individuals who are producing, we find our view becoming more and more limited
to particular habits of individuals rather than directed

[247]

toward human beings as such. As a result, a J-shaped distribution is again superimposed upon the picture, with the mode of the distribution set at that requirement of speed or skill which must be maintained in order that the industry shall keep pace with all the other industries, competitive or coöperative, which make up our industrial system. Now dexterity, speed, endurance, and the like, unlike the acquired habits of driving in traffic, are largely based upon innate or physiological factors. They cannot be readily changed by training or by regulations. How, therefore, can a J-shaped distribution be secured among the working population? The answer is simple but grim. We produce our J-shaped curve in machine industry not by training, but by selection. We can employ only the individuals who by their nature conform, and throw the rest completely out of the economic scheme. In certain industries it seems that this is the very process which is going on today. With the aid of Fig. 9 we can picture what happens in the normal working population through the introduction of organized and technological industry. In the earlier economic era, when manufacture was a handicraft and selling was accomplished through personal relations of producer and consumer, there was a place for nearly everyone. Only a few, comprising the most incompetent (as indicated to the right of line *a* in Fig. 9), were completely excluded. The pattern of economic activities fitted the normal probability distribution of talents fairly well. But machines, with specialization and division of labor, have brought a change. In order to keep the modern large organizations, integrated as units, in operation, there is now required a definite and fairly high minimum requirement below which workers cannot fit into the system. A line, *b*, may therefore be drawn at the mode of the normal distribution curve breaking it into two halves, respectively, those who are acceptable for industry and those who are unacceptable. The latter are now discarded. As the employment of labor-saving machinery increases, and as this fact as well as other conditions of business make fewer employees necessary, the line of demarcation is moved still farther to the left, for example, to the position *c*. And now if we center our atten-

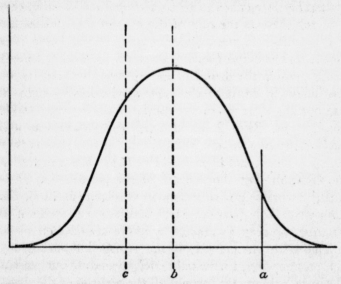

Fig. 9.—A theoretical normal distribution of industrial abilities of a great many workers, showing how the normal distribution may be transformed into a J-shaped distribution by means of selection of only the upper half of the workers. The vertical lines *a*, *b*, and *c* represent a theoretical progressive process of weeding out the workers of lesser efficiency. The right-hand extreme of the curve represents the least efficient and the left-hand extreme the most efficient.

tion upon the workers still retained, we find, in regard to the distribution of their abilities, the true J-shaped curve which has seemed in all our studies to characterize the institutional as contrasted with the purely individual and biological ordering of behavior. This time the J-shaped curve has been achieved not by training the individuals to conform, but by thrusting those who do not conform out of the institutional relationship concerned.

[249]

V

To many readers the analysis of social problems given above will seem to imply a challenge to our whole Western civilization. Our social institutions, many will say, have carried us so far in the direction of progress, and are so unalterably intrenched in all that we call modern life, that to attack them as the root of the evils of this civilization is a hopeless diagnosis indeed. What is the value of a remedy for the evils of society when the use of that remedy would involve the denial of society itself, at least as we now know it? Most of the experts who have sought to cure our ills have given far gentler and more reasonable prescriptions. They have assumed the naturalness and inevitability of economic and political institutions as they have developed, and have tried to adjust human beings to the situation. But the purpose of the present chapter is neither to praise nor condemn, in wholesale fashion, the thing we call civilization. Much less is it my intention to prescribe, or even to predict, a future civilization to be built up when the present one has vanished. Abjuring any such presumption, I have only tried to analyze our present dilemmas, taking into account all the realities of the situation, not merely those described by economists and sociologists, but the facts seen by the psychologists and biologists as well. When all these factors are considered, the problem seems to be more complex than those who seek to solve it through institutional agencies would have us believe. I am not saying that it will be impossible in the future to guide and direct institutional behavior in such a manner as to make life more livable. One cannot foretell the effects of new institutional habits which may be established. It does seem clear, however, that many of the difficulties in the fields we have been discussing have arisen not because we are backward in our development of institutions, but because of the very fact that we *have* institutions at all;

or rather that in trying to meet human needs through institutional alignments we have obscured the reality of the basic biological and psychological character of individuals. This reality, however it may be ignored in social engineering, will probably always remain. To overlook the facts of the distribution of human talents and traits of personality and to assert that the center of reference most important in life is the social system rather than separate individuals, may lead to the development of a social organization of amazing institutional elaboration and efficiency; but it will be sure, in the end, to invite disaster. Whatever our good intentions may be in regard to social planning, cooperation, and organization of effort, we are simply flying in the face of facts if we ignore the curve of distribution upon which individuals, as biological and psychological realities, fall. We make here no pretense that our experiments in the measurement of institutional behavior are anything more than a limited and tentative suggestion. But we are justified in warning the leaders in the management of business, industry, and social planning, that if they are really to substantiate their claim that their efforts are based upon the established principles of science, they must look well to the implications of these differences between the biological distribution curve and the curve of institutionalized behavior. Those experts who are more eager to apply scientific methods to the efficiency of social institutions than to individuals may be making the most unscientific blunder of all.

Hugo Münsterberg took the position that the business of the psychologist was to apply his techniques to the accomplishment of ends which were to be determined by others. It is not the psychologist, he thought, but the industrial, political, or educational leaders of society, working in accordance with social institutions and purposes who should be the mentors of conduct and social policy. In so far as Münsterberg meant that considerations other than those of purely psychological character should determine human ends, there is no denying his position. But the same may be said of the viewpoint of any expert, or for that matter of any social scientist or political or economic leader. Life is too vast and complex to have its objectives determined in any particular department of human endeavor or by any one person or group of persons. In the end only the rank and file of men and women, as whole and integrated individuals, can determine them. And are not psychologists, as men and women, as thoroughly qualified as anyone else? No one's contribution, of course, whether that of psychologist or of social leader, should be considered as more than the revelation of the values of one individual, so far as the ultimate objectives of life are concerned. It seems necessary then to qualify Münsterberg's conception. If psychologists are to be of genuine service in the solution of social problems, they may properly regard their task to lie not merely in showing the means toward the realization of ends dictated by others, but in studying the nature of the ends themselves in so far as they involve the integrity and happiness of individuals. It is the thesis of this chapter that many of our dilemmas result, not from some flaw in the working of institutions, some technical error which industrial, legal, or educational experts can remedy, but from the nature of these institutions themselves, and from the conflict between the attempt to direct life from the standpoint of a perfectly organized social system on the one hand and the personalities of individuals upon the other. If this is true, our problems will never be solved until we can work out some harmony between these two points of view. The task of the psychologist is, through observation and analysis, to make clear this issue and to help in the discovery of methods whereby the conflict and the possible avenues toward its solution may be understood.

INDEX

A

Abnormality, relation to crime, 125
  relation to religion, 136
Accident clinics, case studies, 193*ff*.
  establishment of, 191
Accident proneness, 146, 153*ff*., 192
Accidents, cost of, 146*ff*.
  reaction time as factor in, 151*ff*.
  reduction of, 160
  studies of, in operatives, 147
  susceptibility to, 146, 153*ff*.
Adams, S., 173, 174
Adjustment, vocational, 145*ff*., 247
  significance of work traits in, 154,
    164*ff*.
Adult, education, 77*ff*.
  learning capacity of, and its implica-
    tions, 78*ff*.
Allen, H. H., 151
Allergy, 117
Allport, F. H., 82, 235, 236
Alpert, Augusta, 15
Ambiversion, 26
Anderson, V. V., 158
Anthrax, 118
Aptitude, objective measures of voca-
    tional, 155
  study of practice curves in determina-
    tion of, 164*ff*.
Arithmetic, psychology of, 60*ff*.
Army Alpha Test, 126
Arrington, Ruth E., 19
Ascendance-submission, 225*ff*.
Attention patterning in professional
    men, 112

B

Attitudes, of conformity, 219
  distortions of public, 218
  toward laws, 220
  public *vs*. private, 237
  religious and moral, 234*ff*.
  scales for measuring, 223, 234*ff*.

Baker, S. Josephine, 4
Beaver, Alma Perry, 21
Behavior, of children, with adults, 17
  with other children, 18
  "common-segment" or institutional
    view of, 200*ff*.
  developmental stages of, 7*ff*., 35*ff*.
  economic, segment of, 244*ff*.
  index of institutionalization of, 240*ff*.
  methods of description of, 91*ff*.
  of newborn babe, 7*ff*.
  prediction and control of, 203*ff*.
  resistant, in response to interference,
    22*ff*.
  of six-year-old, 9
  social and emotional, of infants, 16*ff*.
  stereotyping of, 203*ff*.
  time-space recording of, 33*ff*.
  uniform *vs*. diverse, of motorists,
    224*ff*.
Behavior patterns, concept of, 37
Berne, Esther Van Cleve, 20
Binet, Alfred, 3
  test, 48, 58, 59
Bingham, W. V., 192, 197
Blanton, M. S., 17, 29
Blood-pressure records, use of, in
    criminology, 130